THE
IDENTITY
MATRIX

WILLIAM WELLINGTON

ISBN 978-1-63885-840-9 (Paperback)
ISBN 978-1-63885-841-6 (Digital)

Covenant Books
11661 Hwy 707
Murrells Inlet, SC 29576
www.covenantbooks.com

CONTENTS

FOREWORD

I have learned in my lifetime that there is a mysterious force more powerful than belief. I call it "want to believe." People tend to determine their most important beliefs not by observing scientific facts or by personal persuasion, but they mostly believe what they want to believe. I have gone to great effort in this book to present the truth, the whole truth, and nothing but the truth. I believe the Bible is true. Maybe you don't. I have tried to provide supporting evidence to the truths that are presented where practical. I have tried my best to make sure that any speculation or opinion is presented as such. I simply ask right now that you *want to believe* the truth.

INTRODUCTION

Imagine a church staff meeting at the First Church of Anytown, USA. It's probably a Monday or Tuesday morning. The pastor, assistant pastor, and all the church leadership are there discussing the typical things they would be discussing every week—things such as hospital visits, funerals, various maintenance items, and the next special events of the church. These are all good things. There is nothing wrong with anything they are talking about. But suddenly, the people in the meeting notice that the pastor has a laser dot on his forehead. Then another laser dot appears on his forehead. Then all the other people in the staff notice that everyone in the meeting has two laser dots on their foreheads. Each man in the room has two snipers aiming at him. Immediately, the conversation completely changes. This church is in a crossfire. Each of you is also in a crossfire, and you probably don't know it.

My objective is to give you some insight into the crossfire that you are in. You may have the feeling that you are in a spiritual battle, but that you probably are not fully aware that you are in a spiritual crossfire. Multiple issues arise from a crossfire. Not only do you have a firepower issue, but you also have a complicated and confusing defensive situation. One additional attack by your enemy has increased your danger exponentially.

One of Steve Jobs's greatest contributions was leading the development of "apps" that enabled users to interface more easily with complex computer codes and data. I have created a couple of "ideological apps" that will hopefully enable you to understand more easily the spiritual crossfire that you are in.

A valuable tool for analyzing failure events is called Apollo root cause analysis. It is a problem-solving methodology that is based on the Apollo moon landing missions. The first lesson you learn from Apollo root cause analysis is that most humans have a bias that when they see a problem, they attribute that problem to a single root cause. Most problems, however, have multiple root causes. Sometimes, when we start to look at problems in our lives, our families, our organizations, our churches, our work, and our government, we will tend to look for a single root cause. We blame a lot of things such as politicians, sin, and television. All these are legitimate things to look at. But I want to show you how some major root causes are inter-acting and are absolutely wreaking havoc on our lives, our families, our churches, our country, and our world. There are two huge root causes that have us in a crossfire. Let's assemble an "ideological app" that will give you a map of the battlefield which will help you under-stand better what is really going on.

CHAPTER 1

The Personal Identity Matrix

The foundational Bible verse we are going to use is Genesis 1:27.

> So God created man in His own image; in the
> image of God He created him, male and female
> He created them.

Genesis 1:27 is the most foundational verse in the Bible about your identity. In 1905, thousands of years after this verse was written, the XX and XY chromosomes that determine a person's sex were discovered.

Something I like to do is to graph out two variables on a chart. I put the chart below together one morning when I was doing my Saturday morning Bible study. I was feeling that the spiritual and cultural battles other men and I were facing were more complex than I had been thinking. I wanted to see what it would look like if I assumed that there was not only the spiritual war on our personal Christianity in play but also a separate war on each man's masculinity. The chart below is almost exactly what I originally came up with. Once I put this chart on a piece of paper, it was tough for me to think of anything else. It was that enlightening to me. I went back through the Bible, starting with Genesis 1 to see if there was anything else more foundational than this. That's when Genesis 1:27 "jumped out" at me. My chart had followed this verse almost perfectly. It is the exact foundation for what

I am calling the Personal Identity Matrix that we are looking at below. The Personal Identity Matrix below is the "ideological app" that will allow you to evaluate how well you are living according to the way you were made. The Personal Identity Matrix will also help you see both the battlefield and the crossfire that you are in.

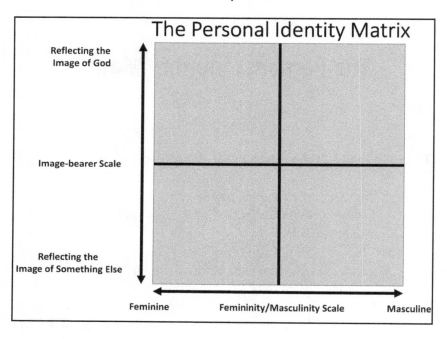

A Quick Start on the Personal Identity Matrix

Let's look at Genesis 1:27 again, and let's look at the Personal Identity Matrix. We have an X-axis that goes from feminine on the left to masculine on the right and a Y-axis which measures how well each of us is reflecting the image of God. There are both physical and spiritual aspects of the Personal Identity Matrix. From conception, we grow physically, but we also change spiritually. You will see the spiritual attributes show up on the matrix as well. Let's look at some examples. The most perfect model of both reflecting the image of God and being perfectly masculine was Jesus Christ. I would also put the pre-fall Adam in the upper right corner. We are going to talk a lot about organizational versus personal masculinity or femininity, but for now, we are going to talk about some organizations. In other words, an organization can "personify" individual traits, and we will measure them as such. We will clarify the definitions a little more as we go along. If you're looking for an organization or an individual that is very masculine but not known for being godly, the best example I could think of is the Hells Angels. I don't think anybody will argue that the Hells Angels or any Hells Angel you meet is both very masculine and also not trying to be godly. They are probably trying to be the opposite of godly. I think most Hells Angels would agree that on the Personal Identity Matrix, they are on the lower right. Now let's head to the far left corner. The best example I found of people who would be very feminine (at least initially) and trying to be ungodly would be any form of Wicca or witchcraft. So I will put them in the lower left corner. Now let's go to the upper left corner. I would put the pre-fall Eve in the upper left with Ruth, Deborah, and some of the great women of God you see in the Bible. As an aside, it's tough to escape the binary of seeing X and Y chromosomes on an X and Y chart. By the time each of us was three years old, we knew that there were four kinds of people, "good boys," "bad boys," "good girls," and "bad girls."

Understanding the Personal Identity Matrix

Before we move forward, let's define a few terms:

a. Matrix

   i.   Something within or from which something else orig-
        inates, develops, or takes form
   ii. A mold from which a relief surface (such as a piece of
        type) is made
   iii. the natural material (such as soil or rock) in which
        something (such as a fossil or crystal) is embedded
   iv. A rectangular array of mathematical elements (such as the
        coefficients of simultaneous linear equations) that can be

combined to form sums and products with similar arrays having an appropriate number of rows and columns

    v.   Something resembling a mathematical matrix, especially in a rectangular arrangement of elements into rows and columns

    vi. Movie *The Matrix* definition: a simulated reality created by thought-capable machines to distract humans while using their bodies as an energy source.

b. Gender and Sex

    i.   Sex: either of the two major forms of individuals that occur in many species and that are distinguished respectively as female or male, especially on the basis of their reproductive organs and structures

    ii. Gender: the behavioral, cultural, or psychological traits typically associated with one sex

c. Are sex and gender the same? It's complicated. Here is what the Merriam-Webster Usage Guide states, "The words sex and gender have a long and intertwined history. In the fifteenth century, gender expanded from its use as a term for a grammatical subclass to join sex in referring to either of the two primary biological forms of a species, meaning sex has had since the fourteenth century; phrases like "the male sex" and "the female gender" are both grounded in uses established for more than five centuries. But in nonmedical and nontechnical contexts, there is no clear delineation, and the status of the words remains complicated. Usage of sex and gender is by no means settled.[1]

d. Identity: who you were, who you are, who you will be, and what you think about those three.

e. Religion: Cambridge Dictionary defines religion as "the belief in and worship of a god or gods or any such system of belief and worship."

---

[1] *Merriam-Webster Dictionary*, online version.

f.   Theology: Cambridge Dictionary defines theology as "a set of beliefs about a particular religion."

g.   Doctrine: Cambridge Dictionary defines doctrine as "a belief or set of beliefs, especially political or religious ones, that are taught and accepted by a particular group."

The Secret History of Masculinity

This section is called the "secret history" because the only kind of masculinity you hear about anymore is "toxic masculinity." Most good things about masculinity have been erased from our culture. In the United States and Western Europe, masculinity (in men) has been under such severe attack that it is at risk of becoming extinct.

Masculinity Traits

In spite of some negative cultural changes that we will describe in future chapters, most people still are able to "know it when they see it" for general masculine traits. Some of these traits are strength, dominance, assertiveness, performance, egotism, money, success, competition, achievement, supporting distinct gender roles, overt, possessing an aptitude for building things, possessing an aptitude for repairing things, and being good at identifying deceptive ideas. These are not all necessarily good things in every context (egotism is a good example), but it's a good general list.

The "best case" masculine traits are the following: strong, protecting, and generous. If you had a good relationship with your father or grandfather, you should have some good memories of your father and/or grandfather exhibiting these traits.

The best definition, history, and analysis of masculinity that I have found come from a book titled *The Church Impotent: The Feminization of Christianity* by Leon J. Podles.[2] Podles says, "The first thing to note is that the female is the norm from which the male must be differentiated. The basic pattern of the human body is roughly female, as one would expect in a mammalian species, and male characteristics develop

---

[2]   Leon J. Podles, *The Church Impotent: The Feminization of Christianity.*

from that pattern only under certain circumstances. 'The female,' says JM Tanner, 'is the basic sex into which embryos develop if not stimulated to do otherwise.' Even the primary sex characteristics of males are produced by the action of androgens on a fetus with female genitals. The presence of nipples on the male body is a constant reminder that the male is a variation on the basic female type."[3]

We often hear that women are more relational than men. Here is another Podles quote, "Masculinity and femininity are characterized, respectively, by separation and communion…"[4]

Another masculine trait is the treatment of risk in life. Podles looked at occupational statistics and found that "men willingly take far more than their share of the risks in society. Of the twenty most dangerous civilian occupations, all but one are almost entirely male. The history of human suffering makes it hard to say whether men or women have suffered more."[5]

Rites of Passage

Another trait of masculinity is the existence in many cultures of a "rite of passage" to symbolize the transition of a boy into manhood. Podles describes the background on these rites, "The ideology of masculinity is founded on biology and psychology but goes beyond them in its cultural manifestations. Simple societies can have an initiatory ritual that recognizes boys as men after they have proved themselves able and willing to confront the dangers of life. More complex societies, on the other hand, give boys no such rites of passage, and they must face every test afresh, not knowing whether they have yet proved themselves men. Initiation entails a sharp break and has a threefold structure: a departure from a previous way of life, a 'liminal' period in which the one being initiated is suspended between two worlds, and the entry into a new way of life."[6]

---

[3]   Ibid. 38.
[4]   Ibid. 41.
[5]   Ibid. 44.
[6]   Ibid. 46.

These rites of passage are important enough to have their own ceremonies in most cultures. The ceremony in the west that we are most familiar with is the Jewish Bar Mitzvah.

Podles continues, "The initiation is completed by rites of incorporation in which the person enters a new way of life, a new world, and assumes a new identity. He is now an initiate and has new knowledge, new powers, new abilities, and new wisdom. He may receive a new name or new clothes to embody his new status. He has been reborn to a greater or lesser degree as a new person."[7]

Here is a table of historical and modern organizations that have had a part in initiating boys into manhood:

	Book of Acts Church	Bar Mitzvah	Military	Fraternal Org.	Occupation	Boy Scouts	Sports	Modern Church	Street Gangs
Risk life for others	•		•		6	•	•		•
Physical struggle or hazing	•		•	•	6	•	•		•
Separation from society	•		•	•	5	•	•		•
Liminal period				•					
Initiation rite	1	•	•	•		•		1	•
Given new powers or religion	•	•	•	•		•			•
Existence of heroes	•	•	•	7		•	•	•	
New name given (identity)	3		•	4					
New clothes given		•	•	•	•	•	•		•
Must pass a series of tests	2	•	•		•	•	•		•
Given new set of rules	•	•	•	•	6	•	•		•
Given new rights and privileges	•	•	•	•	6	•	•	•	•
Social bonding	•	•	•	•	6	•	•	•	•

1. can be Baptism
2. tests are "ad-hoc"
3. Paul was, but not usually
4. some nicknames
5. some occupations such as offshore oil worker
6. depends on occupation
7. some claim historical heroes

Table 1. Organizations with practices that initiate boys into manhood.

---

[7] Ibid. 48.

Note the difference between the historical church described in the book of Acts and the modern church. Also, note how street gangs are a modern alternative for boys looking for a way to become men.

Finally, the ultimate goal of initiating these boys into manhood is to bring them back into society as contributing leaders. Podles describes the final stage, "The boy is finally incorporated into the world of men. Periods of separation and liminality have prepared him for a new life. 'The passivity of neophytes to their instructors, their malleability, which is increased by submission to ordeal, their reduction to a uniform condition are signs of the process whereby they are ground down to be fashioned anew and endowed with additional powers to cope with their new station in life.' The boy is taught the religion of his group, that is, those things that the group regards as sacred and ultimate. Religion in the modern sense is an essential element, perhaps the heart of a masculine initiation. Rosalyn Miles describes this dynamic. 'To be a male is the opposite of being a mother. To be a man, the boy must break away from her, and the further he travels, the greater will be the success of his journey.' He is born again, but this time of man, not of woman. This birth, like the first one, is bloody and violent. 'To make the break, however, the boy has to be constantly encouraged, threatened, thrust forward at every turn and side, and never, never permitted to fall back.' Boys who undergo this transformation have a lifelong bond with all others who have so suffered."[8]

Defining Femininity

To use a modern term, this section needs a "trigger alert" since most Western women have been programmed to have a deep hatred of the roles for which God made them.

The first step in defining femininity is understanding that women are different from men. Anyone will notice one of the major differences immediately. Women are designed to be better looking

---

[8] Ibid. 50.

than men. We are all drawn to beauty, and women are most likely the most beautiful creation of God.

Just like in the previous section about masculinity, in spite of some negative cultural changes that we will describe in future chapters, most people still are able to "know it when they see it" for general feminine traits. Some of these traits are being supportive, caring, relationship-oriented, having gender roles that can overlap (for example, women are able to both have children and provide for their families), and being more covert than overt. Also, women are good at identifying deceptive people (where men are generally stronger at identifying deceptive ideas).

Some other feminine traits are to be caring and generous. Like the previous section, if you had a good relationship with your mother or grandmother, you should have some good memories of your mother and/or grandmother exhibiting these traits.

The best analysis of Christian femininity I have found is a book called *Eve in Exile* by Rebekah Merkle. Merkle goes back to Genesis in a section called "What Are Women Designed For?" Merkle says, "Design matters. The intent of the designer matters."[9]

Merkle goes on to evaluate a key point that I have also been analyzing. Every public school and power institution has adopted the theory of evolution as not a theory but a law. If evolution is true, it means that a lot of what feminists, Marxists, cultural Marxists, etc. are working so hard to accomplish doesn't make any sense at all. They are working in opposition to many of the foundational principles of the theory of evolution, such as survival of the fittest, natural selection, mutation, and random chance. The very existence of morality is a problem for evolutionists, but every evolutionary feminist or Social Justice warrior has a moral code that they are more than willing to cram down your throat. It's sort of humorous to see someone whose existence is defined by being completely enraged at the results of what they consider to be a random process. My own theory is that most evolutionists, like most atheists, don't really believe what they

---

[9] Rebekah Merkle, *Eve in Exile and the Restoration of Femininity*, Canonpress, Moscow, Idaho, 2016.

say they believe. Deep down, they believe in God, and they believe he created the universe. If you don't believe me, please take a break and read Romans 1.

So since I am "preaching to the choir" in this book (I think the choir is big, but not everyone is singing), let's look at what women are designed for. This is important because, according to Merkle, "If God designed women for a specific purpose if there are fixed limits on the feminine nature, then surely, it would follow that when we are living in accordance with those limits and purpose, we will be in our sweet spot. That's where we'll shine, where we'll excel, and where we will find the most fulfillment."[10]

Merkle goes back to Genesis to identify the key purposes seen in the design of women: to subdue, fill, help, and glorify. Again, because of the constant messaging from our culture, looking at the biblical design for women is repulsive to a lot of people, even people who identify as Christian. Remember, it was selfishness that got us into this mess, and selfishness is a big part of the cultural message today. Adam and Eve were created for the purposes described below in Genesis.

> Then the Lord God took the man and put him into the garden of Eden to cultivate it and keep it. (Genesis 2:15)

> Then the Lord God said, "It is not good for the man to be alone; I will make him a helper suitable for him." (Genesis 2:18)

So Eve was created to help Adam to cultivate and keep the Garden of Eden. In Genesis 1:26–28, we see the overall charter for subduing and filling.

> Then God said, "Let Us make man in Our image, according to Our likeness; and let them

---

[10] Ibid. 99.

rule over the fish of the sea and over the birds of the sky and over the cattle and over all the earth, and over every creeping thing that creeps on the earth." God created man in His own image, in the image of God He created him; male and female He created them. God blessed them; and God said to them, "Be fruitful and multiply, and fill the earth, and subdue it; and rule over the fish of the sea and over the birds of the sky and over every living thing that moves on the earth."

This is far more fun and fulfilling than the feminist ideal of women being the queens of their own cubicles. For a much deeper analysis of the God-designed feminine ideal, in particular the part about glorifying, I recommend reading the Merkle book.

In contrast to men, most cultures historically have not had rites of passage for girls to transition into womanhood. However, having children and/or the ability to be a primary caregiver to children has historically been viewed as the major feminine rite(s) of passage.

One of the feminine traits we will be looking at is the desire to seek harmony within groups of people. This feminine trait has been adopted by a lot of men in recent years. This desire for harmony can be so deep that one even tries to please their enemies. As we will see in future chapters, this characteristic can have dangerous consequences.

CHAPTER 2

A Deeper Look at the Personal Identity Matrix

Now that you have a basic understanding of the Personal Identity Matrix, we are going to look at how it can be used to chart and track organizational identities. We will look at false identity structures, how forces are trying to move you around the matrix, and how, ultimately, this will all play out.

Personal versus Organizational Masculinity or Femininity

Before we move forward, let's take a deeper look at individual versus organizational masculinity or femininity. This is important but can be confusing, so let's revisit.

Here are some spectrums that show feminine and masculine organizational traits (feminine trait is on the left, masculine is on the right):

Organization	Feminine	Masculine
Work	Support Group	Make Money
Church	Counseling	Mission Work
School	Pep Rally	Acquire Skills and Knowledge
Family	Single Parent (Female)	One Male and One Female Parent
Military	Double Standards	Tough Standards
Sports	Participation Trophy	Single Winner

Table 2. Spectrum of organizations that can personify feminine or masculine traits.

Notice that on the family metric, the traditional nuclear family is shown as more masculine. While that is obvious since it is being compared to a single-parent home headed by a female (statistically, this is the most common single-parent situation), organizations that have distinct gender roles are measured as more masculine. We will explain that more in the next section.

Let's say we have two groups. Each group consists of 50% males, 50% females. Is there a way we can gauge the overall masculinity or femininity of that group? I've done a lot of international business over the course of my career. There are professors in universities and colleges that study international business. They measure different characteristics for each culture they study. A major cultural parameter is whether gender roles are either clearly defined or loosely defined. For example, I used to have a job where I lived in Minnesota and would fly down to support one of our facilities in Puerto Rico. In Puerto Rico, if one of the women in the factory office became pregnant, she was almost not expected to do any more work for the next year. They let her just sit in a cubicle and prop her feet up, and that was about all they expected from her. Then I would get on a plane and fly back to Minnesota, and there's the wife and mom at the house two doors down from me push mowing her yard with a severe limp because she had a sprained ankle. So Puerto Rico has more clearly defined gender roles. The culture in Minnesota had smeared the gender roles so that they are more loosely defined. Let me give you a thought experiment for organizational masculinity or femininity that I've chosen because the math works out easily. The world record for men's bench press (with the special bench-press shirt they wear), it's hard to believe, but it's about 1,000 pounds. The world record for women (with the same type of shirt) is around 500 pounds. That's amazing too. But looking at the Personal Identity Matrix, let's say all the men decide to become as feminized as they can be, and all the women decide to be as masculine as they can be. Can we just say "No problem," the men will take over the women's roles and the women take over the men's roles? Look what happens to the overall strength of that organization. Nobody will be bench-pressing 1,000 pounds anymore. Some of the women will bench-press 500 pounds, but the overall strength of that culture or that group has decreased. I would call that a more feminine culture when the gender roles become switched or confused. This means that an organization or culture with distinct gender roles (masculine men and feminine women) is stronger, more synergistic, and more masculine than an egalitarian one.

True Identity versus False Identity

There are primary, secondary, tertiary, and so on components of every person's identity. Based on the order that these components are presented in Genesis, here is when they appear:

1) Image of God (Genesis 1:26 and 27)
2) Male or female (Genesis 1:27)
3) Family (Genesis 1:28)
4) Dominion or work (Genesis 1:28, 2:15)
5) Obedience (Genesis 2:17)
6) Name (Genesis 2:20)

7) Geographic location (Genesis 4:16)
8) Language (Genesis 10:5, 11:7)
9) Nations (Genesis 10:5)
10) Beauty (Genesis 12:11)
11) Jew or Gentile (Genesis 16)

Here are some other personal identity components. Most of these can be good, bad, or neutral, depending on how they are emphasized:

1) Personal wealth
2) Social status
3) Skin color
4) Looks
5) Power
6) Job performance
7) Whom do you love? (sports teams, for example)
8) Whom do you hate?
9) Victim (or perceived victim) of oppression or suffering
10) Behavior
11) Addictions

A simple way to explain the "workings" of the Personal Identity Matrix is to use what I call the "Alabama Man Identity Matrix." If you showed this chart to a group of men in Alabama, almost all of them would *identify* with one of the four quadrants. The two axes (Alabama/Auburn and Ford/Chevy) obviously do not completely define the identity of all men in Alabama, but these are important descriptors to them that can impact the "tribes" that these men are accepted into and socialize with.

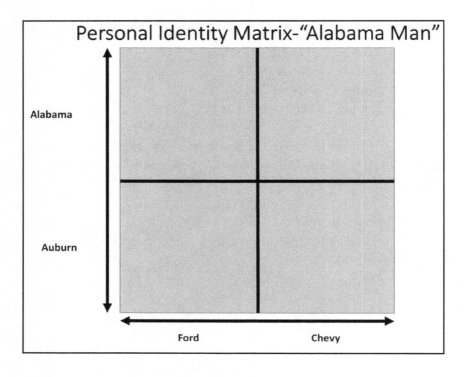

A lot of larger towns and smaller cities have large numbers of people whose actions indicate they are operating on the false and deceptive Socialite Identity Matrix shown below. I saw a bumper sticker on a BMW in a wealthy section of Columbia, South Carolina, once that said, "He Who Dies with the Most Toys Wins." The objective of the socialite is to move as far as possible into the upper right of the Socialite Identity Matrix. The money axis (X-axis) is a little easier for people to measure since it's difficult for a broke person to pretend for long that they have money. The social status axis (Y-axis) is tougher to quantify. Politicians and leaders of banks and various civic groups are generally regarded as having social status. People who come from wealthy or powerful families are also regarded highly on the social status scale. People who operate on the Socialite Identity Matrix are somewhat likely to attend church, but they will tend to choose a church that is regarded as an organization with high social status or at least a church that has a few people there with money and/or power.

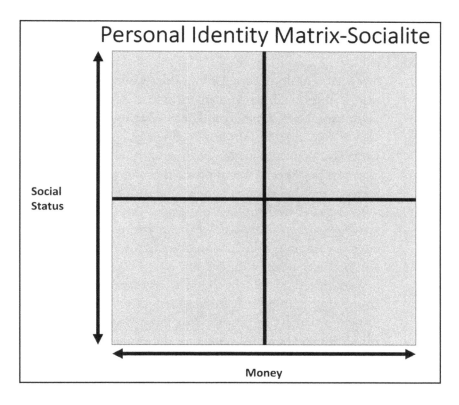

The people in the upper right corner, with high social status and a lot of money, can be bound by a lot of unwritten social rules. If their mom or their wife says they are wearing the wrong outfit, they cannot even make it out the front door. A person with a lot of money but low social status might be called "eccentric" by people who operate in this matrix. The people in the lower right corner with high money and low social status have the most freedom and probably the most fun. This is why "Duck Dynasty" was so popular. The Robertsons have plenty of money, but they did not have much social status before they made their money. The result is that they can afford to do just about whatever they want, and they are not hindered by concerns of what other people might think.

The people in the lower left are labeled weird, losers, lazy, or stupid and are rejected from the "club" altogether.

This false identity matrix has resulted in a lot of Christians being shunned for the wrong reasons.

> My brethren, do not hold your faith in our glorious Lord Jesus Christ with an attitude of personal favoritism. For if a man comes into your assembly with a gold ring and dressed in fine clothes, and there also comes in a poor man in dirty clothes, and you pay special attention to the one who is wearing the fine clothes, and say, "You sit here in a good place," and you say to the poor man, "You stand over there, or sit down by my footstool," have you not made distinctions among yourselves, and become judges with evil motives? Listen, my beloved brethren: did not God choose the poor of this world to be rich in faith and heirs of the kingdom which He promised to those who love Him? But you have dishonored the poor man. Is it not the rich who oppress you and personally drag you into court? Do they not blaspheme the fair name by which you have been called? If, however, you are fulfilling the royal law according to the Scripture, "You shall love your neighbor as yourself," you are doing well. But if you show partiality, you are committing sin and are convicted by the law as transgressors. For whoever keeps the whole law and yet stumbles in one point, he has become guilty of all. For He who said, "Do not commit adultery," also said, "Do not commit murder." Now if you do not commit adultery, but do commit murder, you have become a transgressor of the law. So speak and so act as those who are to be judged by the law of liberty. For judgment will be merciless to one who has shown no mercy; mercy triumphs over judgment. (James 2:1–13)

People who are high on the socialite scale have usually invested heavily of their time, talent, and treasure to build relationships with people who are deemed to be of high social status. Anyone who is lower on the social status and/or money scale is regarded as a potential threat to these relationships and will be rejected. Sometimes, it gets nasty. If you hear stories or rumors of a man who is highly regarded in a church but secretly paid for his daughter to have an abortion, it probably means he was trying to stay in the "club." As American Express used to say, "Membership has its privileges."

The "Hollywood" Personal Identity Matrix is like the Socialite Personal Identity Matrix but is more likely to be associated with bad behavior. It is loosely described by Billy Joel in his song "It's Still Rock and Roll to Me." "Don't you know about the new fashion, honey? All you need are looks and a whole lotta money…" People operating on the Hollywood Identity Matrix are thinking beyond their hometown. You usually won't meet many of these people, but you will see them on TV.

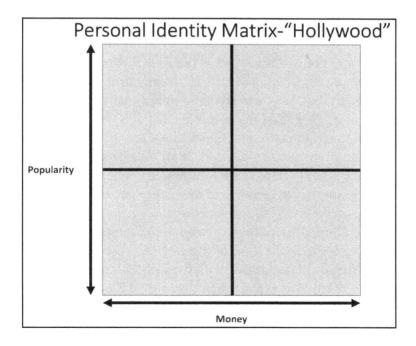

How you rank order your identity traits will not only determine which identity matrix you are attempting to operate in, but it will also determine which "tribe" you are a part of.

The true Personal Identity Matrix is the one based on Genesis 1:27, "So God created man in His own image; in the image of God He created him, male and female He created them." In other words, the top two characteristics that determine your identity are how well you are reflecting the image of God and how well you are reflecting masculinity if you are male and femininity if you are female. Of course, we cannot hope to spiritually reflect the image of God without being born again through Jesus Christ. We also have the option of trying to build our identities around things that are less important than the foundational image-ness or male-ness (I am talking to men here). For example, we can try to base our identity on how big of an Atlanta Falcons fan we are, but ultimately, the true Personal Identity Matrix will prevail. We are going to explore in this book the spiritual war on your identity. Isn't it interesting that on Halloween, which is the most revered day for Satanists, they celebrate by dressing up like something they are not? It is an intentional attack on God-given identity.

The thesis of this book is that not only is Satan trying to move men down on the Personal Identity Matrix from being godly to being ungodly, but he is also trying to move men left on this matrix to be less masculine and more feminine. Satan is also trying to move women from feminine to masculine. Those are the two laser dots in the crossfire from the introduction. If an organization can be feminized, it is less likely to fight back if someone tries to destroy it. The primary groups that are being used to accomplish these moves are the feminists and the LGBTQ movement.

Masculinity physically starts with a Y chromosome. I'm not an expert on biology, maybe some of you are, but every human has twenty-three pairs of chromosomes that physically define who we are. On one of the twenty-three pairs, men have a Y chromosome; women do not. It's a foundational difference. Bruce Jenner can never change that. Both axes on the Personal Identity Matrix start with genetics and then move to behavior. You see it very quickly in Genesis during the fall. One can make a case that even before the fall or concurrent with the fall, Adam and Eve had started to drift toward the center with their masculine and feminine roles before they fell.

Here is the "fully populated" Personal Identity Matrix:

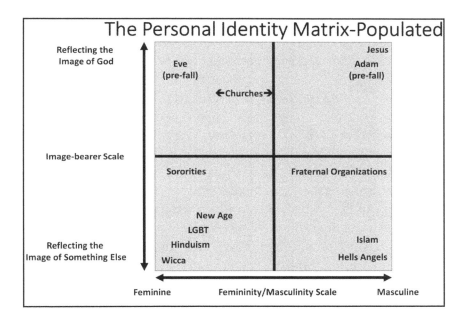

I am convinced that all of us men start off in life somewhere in the neighborhood of where the Hells Angels are due to our fallen nature. I remember when my oldest son was about two or three, he had been watching me light a grill with some matches and damp charcoal. It took me several tries to get the grill to light. The problem was my son was paying attention. The next day, he found some matches and decided to build a campfire in his bed. Everybody was okay, but there was a lot of smoke damage. It could have been worse, but some very brave firemen who showed up put the fire out and threw the bed out the second-story window. We were dealing with the aftermath of all this, and a week or two later, I was helping in the church nursery. I'm having this Norman Rockwell moment in a nice comfortable rocking chair. It's all cushiony, and I am holding one or two babies while I am watching the kids play. Then I saw my son crawl over to another boy. There is a big pile of toys in the middle of the floor, and the kids can walk or crawl around to whichever toy they want to play with. My son crawls over to another little boy in front of me who was playing with a toy. My son looks at the little boy and says, "Hand me that toy, or I'll burn down your house." So that's a small young man with some extreme Hells Angels tendencies already. I think most men start somewhere in that neighborhood on the chart.

The War on Sexual Identity

In a recent (1/22/20) interview, Green Bay Packers quarter-back Aaron Rodgers said about changing his religious beliefs from Christianity, "Ultimately, it was that rules and regulations, and binary systems don't really resonate with me." He went on by saying, "Religion can be a crutch. It can be something that people have to have to make themselves feel better." Rodgers continued, "Because it's set up binary, it's us and them, saved and unsaved, heaven and hell. It's enlightened and heathen. It's holy and righteous…that makes a lot of people feel better about themselves."[11]

If you summarize Rodgers's philosophy, it's that binary is bad. Therefore, "not binary" is good. There is already a logical problem here. "Binary is bad" versus "not-binary is good" is binary. In a supposed attempt to run from binary, Rodgers ended up back at binary.

There is something deeper than a rebellion against God going on here. Binary is baked into some parts of the created order to such a degree that the war on a created binary becomes a war on reality.

---

[11] https://people.com/sports/aaron-rodgers-opens-up-about-religion-to-danica-patrick-i-dont-know-how-you-can-believe-in-a-god/.

State 1	State 2	Reference
Light	Darkness	Genesis 1:4
Waters Above	Waters Under	Genesis 1:6-8
Earth	Seas	Genesis 1:9-10
Man	Woman	Genesis 1:27
Good	Evil	Genesis 3:5

Table 3. Created entities with designed-in binary.

Anyone who tries to defend or maintain one of these boundaries is instantly called a name. The name you are called depends on which boundary you are defending. In a future chapter, we will talk about how our modern culture wants to put you in "label jail" for telling the truth about the boundaries.

Leon Podles, in *The Church Impotent,* writes, "God does not leave the universe an undifferentiated chaos. He, as creator, separates light from darkness, the waters above the earth from the waters below the earth. He creates the sun and moon and stars to separate time into discrete intervals. He creates mankind, male and female, and creates Eve by separating her from Adam. For this reason, 'a man leaves his mother and father, and the two become one flesh,' the narrator explains. In marriage, man imitates God by following the pattern first of separation and in union. The separation is for the sake of the union, but the action of separation dominates in the man."[12]

Where does modern culture say you start on this (Personal Identity Matrix) chart? Modern culture is going to try to ignore your chromosomes and put you right in the middle of the chart. Then modern culture will tell you that you can move wherever you want on this chart, and the way you are "engineered" does not matter.

Let's go back to the Personal Identity Matrix. One of the most profound spiritual journeys in the Bible is in the book of Acts, where we watch the spiritual journey of where Saul became Paul. I'm convinced that Saul started off in the lower right corner and was on a

[12] Leon Podles, *The Church Impotent-The Feminization of Christianity* (Dallas, TX: Spence Publishing Company, 1999), 62.

path where he was transformed to the upper right corner. We should all aspire to end up there. But let's do some trigonometry for a minute. Where would you put the "drag queen" RuPaul on this chart? I say lower left. I don't think it's a big argument. Who has the farther distance to travel on the chart to be a masculine image-bearer of God, Saul or RuPaul? It's RuPaul.

The War on Your Personal Identity

The endgame of the war on personal identity has two parts: the first is to erase gender differences, and the second is to erase the image of God from every human. This is the crossfire we described at the beginning of the book. Exactly what erasing gender differences will look like has yet to be determined. As of now, there is increasing gender chaos, and it is becoming less and less socially acceptable to be a feminine female or a masculine male. Feminists have not promoted femininity in females. They have done the opposite. To completely erase the image of God from a person, that person must, by definition, cease to exist. That is the real reason totalitarian regimes have perpetrated mass murder. But we will get to that a little later.

Moving Personal Identity to Group Identity

One of the consequences of feminizing a culture is that when masculinity is gone, there is a loss of individualism. That is because individualism is a masculine trait. This loss of masculinity sets up the whole culture for collectivism. Marxists cannot emotionally handle individual achievement, so they are trying to take advantage of the loss of individualism. People are afraid of being identified as a person, so they feel more secure if they are part of a group. They would rather fail as part of a group than succeed as an individual. This also sets up a culture for Identity Politics and Cultural Marxism. Toxically feminized people are all about seeking out victim support groups that they can belong to.

George Orwell describes dystopian collectivism in *1984*, "In principle, a Party member had no spare time and was never alone except in bed. It was assumed that when he was not working, eating, or sleeping, he would be taking part in some kind of communal recreations. To do anything that suggested a taste for solitude, even to go for a walk by yourself, was slightly dangerous. There was a word for it in Newspeak, *ownlife*, it was called, meaning individualism and eccentricity."[13]

In 2012, Barak Obama made his infamous "you didn't build that" speech. "There are a lot of wealthy, successful Americans who agree with me because they want to give something back," the president said. "If you've been successful, you didn't get there on your own. You didn't get there on your own. I'm always struck by people who think, well, it must be because I was just so smart. There are a lot of smart people out there. It must be because I worked harder than everybody else. Let me tell you something—there are a whole bunch of hardworking people out there. If you were successful, somebody along the line gave you some help. There was a great teacher somewhere in your life. Somebody helped to create this unbelievable American system that we have that allowed you to thrive. Somebody invested in roads and bridges. *If you've got a business, you didn't build that. Somebody else made that happen*," he said. "The Internet didn't get invented on its own. Government research created the Internet so that all the companies could make money off the Internet."

Notice how triggered Obama seemed by the concept of individual achievement. We will explore the motives for that in future sections.

Our primary group identity should be determined by whom we will spend forever with. You need to learn to get along with that group now if you are going to be with them forever. So be extremely careful about which "team" you join.

---

[13] George Orwell, *1984* (Harcourt Brace and Company), 84.

Ultimate Identity

The Bible tells us how people will ultimately be judged. It's sobering, and it's binary.

> When the thousand years are completed, Satan will be released from his prison and will come out to deceive the nations which are in the four corners of the earth, Gog and Magog, to gather them together for the war; the number of them is like the sand of the seashore. And they came up on the broad plain of the earth and surrounded the camp of the saints and the beloved city, and fire came down from heaven and devoured them. And the devil who deceived them was thrown into the lake of fire and brimstone, where the beast and the false prophet are also; and they will be tormented day and night forever and ever. Then I saw a great white throne and Him who sat upon it, from whose presence earth and heaven fled away, and no place was found for them. And I saw the dead, the great and the small, standing before the throne, and books were opened; and another book was opened, which is the book of life; and the dead were judged from the things which were written in the books, according to their deeds. And the sea gave up the dead which were in it, and death and Hades gave up the dead which were in them; and they were judged, every one of them according to their deeds. Then death and Hades were thrown into the lake of fire. This is the second death, the lake of fire. And if anyone's name was not found written in the book of life, he was thrown into the lake of fire. (Revelation 21:7–15)

It is crucial that you get your identity right. Individually, you must reflect the image of God and function the way you were designed, but it is also crucial that you belong to the right group eternally. Some liberal theologian is not going to bake some cookies and sit God and Satan down at the kitchen table and work out a compromise.

CHAPTER 3

The Political Identity Matrix

We have seen in the Bible how personal identity is based on being made in the image of God and whether we are male or female. Personal identity is foundational because it is obviously impossible to have a group without individuals. But people grew into families, and families grew into nations. Individual identity tends to be more masculine. Group identity tends to be more feminine, although that is not always the case. Where people are on the Personal Identity Matrix has a major impact on their group identity and political views.

Family Identity

There is plenty of biblical evidence that the family is the God-ordained structure to raise children. But that's not the only place you have to look. One of the slogans you see in automobile advertising is "form follows function." You don't have to be a theologian or scientist to see that one man and one woman have been designed to produce a child. Women have been designed to feed a baby. A father has been designed to both protect and provide for a child. A father has also been designed to both model correct behavior and teach a boy. A mother has been designed to both model correct behavior and teach a girl. But our culture is now so "progressive" that to do anything but pretend that this form that follows function is obsolete is to invite outrage and cancellation.

There are a couple of things about family identity that are often overlooked. One is that families historically have taken the name of the father. This is obviously (gasp) patriarchal. The second is that the name is often derived from the occupation of the father. For example, *Smith* came from *blacksmith*. *Miller* meant someone who worked in a mill, and *Baker* is obvious. Many European last names have the "son of" origins, such as *Johnson* or *Jackson*. Another historical marker of family identity is a crest or coat of arms. These emblems were originally used to identify soldiers who were hidden behind a helmet or a shield in battle. These crests typically have symbolic colors and pictures and have a unique family motto, such as the Kelly family's "Turris Mortis Mihi Deus," meaning "God is my tower."

One of the objectives listed on the original Black Lives Matter (BLM) website is "We disrupt the Western-prescribed nuclear family structure requirement by supporting each other as extended families and 'villages' that collectively care for one another, especially our children, to the degree that mothers, parents, and children are comfortable."[14] It may surprise you that to BLM, Black families don't matter very much.

God's Nation from Personal Identity to National Identity

The first occurrence of the word "nation" in the Bible happens right before the Tower of Babel.

> These are the families of the sons of Noah, according to their genealogies, by their nations; and out of these nations were separated on the earth after the flood. (Genesis 10:32)

---

[14] https://www.foxnews.com/us/blm-deletes-page-disruption-nuclear-family.

In Genesis 11, we see the first experiment in globalism and how it was cleverly destroyed by God.

> Now the whole earth used the same language and the same words. It came about as they journeyed east, that they found a plain in the land of Shinar and settled there. They said to one another, "Come, let us make bricks and burn them thoroughly." And they used brick for stone, and they used tar for mortar. They said, "Come, let us build for ourselves a city, and a tower whose top will reach into heaven, and let us make for ourselves a name, otherwise we will be scattered abroad over the face of the whole earth." The Lord came down to see the city and the tower which the sons of men had built. The Lord said, "Behold, they are one people, and they all have the same language. And this is what they began to do, and now nothing which they purpose to do will be impossible for them. Come, let Us go down and there confuse their language, so that they will not understand one another's speech." So the Lord scattered them abroad from there over the face of the whole earth; and they stopped building the city. Therefore its name was called Babel, because there the Lord confused the language of the whole earth; and from there the Lord scattered them abroad over the face of the whole earth.

Genesis 11 finishes with the genealogy from Shem that leads to Abram (to be known as Abraham in the future). In Genesis 12, we see the Lord speak to Abram in verses 1–3:

> Now the Lord said to Abram,
> Go from your country,
> And from your relatives

And from your father's house,
To the land which I will show you;
And I will make you into a great nation,
And I will bless you,
And make your name great;
And you shall be a blessing;
And I will bless those who bless you,
And the one who curses you I will curse.
And in you all the families of the earth will be
blessed.

Genesis continues as Abraham's descendants continue to multiply. Then we see the foundations of a new nation being formed in Exodus 18:19–23 when Jethro spoke to Moses:

Now listen to me: I will give you counsel, and God be with you. You be the people's representative before God, and you bring the disputes to God, then admonish them about the statutes and the laws, and make known to them the way in which they are to walk and the work they are to do. Furthermore, you shall select out of all the people able men who fear God, men of truth, those who hate dishonest gain; and you shall place these over them as leaders of thousands, of hundreds, of fifties, and of tens. Let them judge the people at all times; and let it be that they will bring to you every major matter, but they will judge every minor matter themselves. So it will be easier for you, and they will carry the burden with you. If you do this thing and God so commands you, then you will be able to endure, and all these people also will go to their places in peace.

God further charters the new nation in Exodus 19:4–6.

> And Moses went up to God, and the Lord called to him from the mountain, saying, "This is what you shall say to the house of Jacob and tell the sons of Israel: 'You yourselves have seen what I did to the Egyptians, and how I carried you on eagles' wings, and brought you to Myself. Now then, if you will indeed obey My voice and keep My covenant, then you shall be My own possession among all the peoples, for all the earth is Mine; and you shall be to Me a kingdom of priests and a holy nation.' These are the words that you shall speak to the sons of Israel."

So in spite of "nationalism" being a dirty word in our culture and "globalism" being celebrated, we see at the Tower of Babel that God destroyed globalism to build nations. Then we see how God built a special nation from Abraham.

The Political Spectrum

Merriam Webster defines politics as "the art or science of government" or "the art or science concerned with guiding or influencing governmental policy." MW defines political as "of or relating to government or the conduct of government." It also defines government as "the body of persons that constitutes the governing authority of a political unit or organization such as the officials comprising the governing body of a political unit and constituting the organization as an active agency..."

In the book *Ruler of the Nations*[15] by Gary DeMar, the introduction by Gary North describes a structure that can be used to analyze any contractual institution, whether it be an ecclesiastical covenant, civil government, or even a family. This structure is first seen in the Bible in the book of Deuteronomy. Here it is with related questions on the right:

Biblical Covenant Structure	Related Question
The transcendence and immanence of God	Who's in charge here?
Authority/hierarchy of God's covenant	To whom do I report?
Biblical law/ethics/dominion	What are the rules?
Judgement/oath: blessings and cursings	What happens to me if I obey (or disobey)?
Continuity/inheritance	Does this outfit have a future?

Table 4. Biblical covenant structure.

The media often describes a "political spectrum." The spectrum is rarely analyzed in-depth, and it is almost intentionally confusing. For example, "Antifa" means "anti-fascist," and there is not much argument that they are "leftists" and that the fascists are from the right side of the spectrum. To give you an idea of how confusing the standard political spectrum is, here is a comparison of two regimes that are assumed to be opposites, Nazi Germany and the current (2021) People's Republic of China:

	Nazi Germany	People's Republic of China
Form of Government	Fascist	Communist
Nationalism vs. Internationalism	Nationalism	Nationalism
Property Ownership	Hybrid	Hybrid
Racial separation	persecuted Jews	persecute Uyghurs
Socialism vs. Personal Freedom	Socialism	Socialism
Religion	Working toward a pagan / Christianity syncretism	Officially athiest
Social Hierarchy vs Egalitarianism	Social Hierarchy	Trending toward egalitarianism

Table 5. Comparing the political systems of PRC and Nazi Germany.

[15] Gary DeMar, *Ruler of the Nations* (Fort Worth, TX: Dominion Press, 1987).

So two regimes that are assumed to be opposite are, in reality, remarkably similar. So we can see that the political "spectrum" is a deeply flawed way to view politics.

From a Spectrum to the Political Identity Matrix

As I worked with the Personal Identity Matrix, I thought it explained personal identity dynamics very well, but it didn't fully explain what I saw happening with group identities and political struggles. So I wondered if the same thing was happening with politics. Was everyone only looking at one variable when two variables would better explain the situation?

Let's apply the "app" of a matrix to the political spectrum the same way we did with personal identity. After much research and trial and error, I determined that the two major variables that describe political structure are 1) the degree of state control and 2) the degree of social hierarchy in an organization. Here is what it looks like, fully populated:

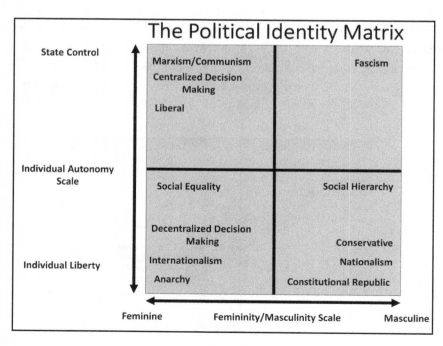

What I found was that Marxism/communism and fascism both are socialistic, but fascism is the masculine form of socialism. Marxism and communism are the feminine forms of socialism. Or, more precisely, fascism is the patriarchal form of socialism, and communism is the matriarchal form of socialism.

The ultimate difference between communism and fascism would be that Marxism/communism/socialism promotes globalism while fascism is nationalistic.

Benito Mussolini said that "war is to man what maternity is to a woman. From a philosophical and doctrinal viewpoint, I do not believe in perpetual peace."[16] Mussolini was a totalitarian like any of the Marxist or Communist dictators are, but you would never see a slogan like that associated with the Communist Party.

---

[16] https://www.brainyquote.com/quotes/benito_mussolini_143479.

CHAPTER 4

The Endgame—Where Satan Is Trying to Move You

Christians have been given a valuable gift, the gift of biblical prophecy. This gift of prophecy is invaluable because it tells us the endgame of Satan. If you see someone trying to take you to the same place that Satan is, you should resist, not follow, that person. The most comprehensive end times prophecy is in Revelation.

> Then I saw another beast coming up out of the earth; and he had two horns like a lamb, and he spoke as a dragon. He exercises all the authority of the first beast in his presence. And he makes the earth and those who live on it worship the first beast, whose fatal wound was healed. He performs great signs, so that he even makes fire come down out of the sky to the earth in the presence of people. And he deceives those who live on the earth because of the signs which it was given him to perform in the presence of the beast, telling those who live on the earth to make an image to the beast who had the wound of the sword and has come to life. And it was given to him to give breath to the image of the beast, so that the image of the beast would even

speak and cause all who do not worship the image of the beast to be killed. And he causes all, the small and the great, the rich and the poor, and the free and the slaves, to be given a mark on their right hands or on their foreheads, and he decrees that no one will be able to buy or to sell, except the one who has the mark, either the name of the beast or the number of his name. Here is wisdom. Let him who has understanding calculate the number of the beast, for the number is that of a man; and his number is [n]six hundred and sixty-six. (Revelation 13:11–18)

There is a parallel passage in Daniel 7:25.

And he will speak against the Most High and wear down the saints of the Highest One, and he will intend to make alterations in times and in law; and they will be handed over to him for a time, times, and half a time.

Matthew 24:3–13 also describes the end times.

And as He was sitting on the Mount of Olives, the disciples came to Him privately, saying, "Tell us, when will these things happen, and what will be the sign of Your coming, and of the end of the age?" And Jesus answered and said to them, "See to it that no one misleads you. For many will come in My name, saying, 'I am the Christ,' and they will mislead many people. And you will be hearing of wars and rumors of wars. See that you are not alarmed, for those things must take place, but that is not yet the end. For nation will rise against nation, and kingdom against kingdom, and there will be famines and earthquakes in various places.

But all these things are merely the beginning of birth pains. Then they will hand you over to tribulation and kill you, and you will be hated by all nations because of My name. And at that time many will fall away, and they will betray one another and hate one another. And many false prophets will rise up and mislead many people. And because lawlessness is increased, most people's love will become cold. But the one who endures to the end is the one who will be saved. This gospel of the kingdom shall be preached in the whole world as a testimony to all the nations, and then the end will come."

The prophecy above shows Satan's endgame, which is shown in the far right column of the chart below. The endgame is a worldwide dictatorship that will have near-total control over civil government, finance, and religion. The interim steps are interpolated in the "Disorder" column.

System	Biblical Order	Disorder	New World Order
Financial	Coined money	Debt-based paper money	Mark on the hand
Civil government	Nations	Erase national borders	One world government
Personal government	Law (self-control)	Lawlessness	Dictatorship
Family government	Nuclear family	Sexual anarchy	"Equality"
Church government	Decentralized churches	Denominations	Reclamation into New World Religion

Table 6. Current order to disorder to the New World Order.

The organizations that are working on moving the world from Biblical order to disorder are the anarchists (Antifa), Marxists (BLM), LGBTQ groups, central banks, and corrupted seminaries.

The organizations that plan on moving the world from disorder to the New World Order are the secret societies (Masons, Shriners, etc.) and globalist groups like the World Economic Forum.

Now that we have explored biblical order, Satan's endgame, and the interim state (disorder), we know the general path along which evil cultural forces want to move you. In the next few chapters, we will analyze some of the tactics of the enemy to move you down that path.

The Real Karl Marx

Marxism is often presented as strictly an economic system that is "nicer" or "more just" because it ostensibly redistributes wealth from rich people to poor people. But Marxism (known as Classical Marxism when described in strictly economic terms) cannot be fully understood unless we study its founder, Karl Marx.

Karl Marx said, "The idea of God is the keynote of a perverted civilization. It must be destroyed." He also said, "I wish to avenge myself against the One who rules above."[17] Notice the contradiction of those two statements. The first statement is atheistic. But the second statement clearly shows that Marx is not really an atheist. He actually hates God.

Let's look at the spiritual aspects of Marxism. It's obviously an example of people supposedly having faith in something that does not work.

Officially, Marxism claims to be atheistic. It is debated as to whether any atheist really is an atheist or if they are just trying to ignore God because they hate Him. There is strong evidence that Marx was a Satan worshipper and even stronger evidence that Marx believed in the existence of God, so for any Marxist or Marxist government to claim to be atheist is being disingenuous to true Marxism.

The unpublicized ideological foundation of Marxism is that God is the "oppressor" and that Satan is the "oppressed."

---

[17]   Richard Wurmbrand, *Marx and Satan* (Westchester, IL: Crossway Books).

Peter Hammond, a missionary in Africa, tells the story of Christians being tortured by Marxists. At some point, the Christians asked the Marxists why they didn't stop torturing them and just kill them. The Marxists replied, "If we kill you, you will go to heaven. What we want is for you to renounce your faith and go to hell with us."

When you see that someone is as evil as Karl Marx, it is imperative to question the motives of absolutely everything he said, wrote, or did. People like Marx are addicted to evil, and like their father the devil, love to deceive people.

To summarize the motives of Karl Marx, he was energized by two things. One is a hatred of God, and the second is a hatred of the right to private ownership of property.

I was surprised at how big of a deal identity was to Marxists. Brannon Howse says in Marxianity, "The Frankfurt school set about to destroy the perceived differences between masculinity and femininity. Does that go on today? Absolutely. And by destroying the American male, cultural Marxists knew they could create a bigger government, the ultimate goal of Marxism."[18]

In future sections about Cultural Marxism and Critical Race Theory, you will see why it is not often discussed that Karl Marx was a straight White male.

Marxism
A Satanic Bait and Switch

It is not unusual for things to work better in theory than in practice. But the gap between the Marxism taught on college campuses and the Marxism practiced by totalitarian regimes is so large that it can be called a "bait and switch" or, more accurately, an evil deception. Millions of dollars have been spent in American universities trying to make Marxism work on paper. But it has never worked in practice. Only when Marxist (essentially Communist) countries

---

[18] Brannon S. House, *Marxianity* (Collierville, TN: Worldview Weekend Press, 2018), 11–12.

incorporate some features of capitalism do they have any success at all.

Economics 101

Marxism preys on covetous people who do not understand economics. Since Marxism is based on faulty economic assumptions, we need to take a brief look at economics. Merriam-Webster defines economics as "a social science concerned chiefly with description and analysis of the production, distribution, and consumption of goods and services." Human wants are essentially unlimited, so we will focus on production and distribution. Economics is the study of where supply meets demand. Meeting demand with supply is the purpose of business.

A foundational principle of economics that is often misunderstood is that wealth must be created. There is a general consensus that there are four ways to create wealth: fishing, farming, mining, and manufacturing. In each case, human beings interact with raw materials to add value to create and distribute a finished product. The universe is designed to inherently reward efficiency and punish inefficiency. Factories, farms, ships, and mines are dynamic systems that are constantly looking for breakthrough ideas to improve efficiency or quality. Looking at economics as a whole, the more food, clothing, shelter, medical technology, transportation, etc. that is produced on a per capita basis, the wealthier that economic system will be. The wealthiest economies usually do a good job of rewarding people for both high production and good ideas. The system that does the best job of creating a wealthy economy is capitalism.

The other metric that should be used to evaluate an economy is the level of success it has in meeting the needs of people. For example, capitalism does a great job of getting someone open-heart surgery quickly and safely. No other system can compete with that. Yet Marxists will focus on the fact that a cardiologist makes more money than a trash collector. The fact that in a capitalist country, a cardiologist makes more money than a trash collector is one of the primary reasons that you are far better off having a heart attack in a capitalist country than in a Marxist country. People who help the most people or perform the most difficult or dangerous tasks should earn the most money, and capitalism does a good job of doing that.

Nobody has a moral right to eat someone else's seed corn. That's actually immoral and hurts everyone. But Marxists believe that anyone with a perceived need has a right to eat another person's seed corn.

The Bait

Two major characteristics of masculinity are individualism and competition, which are also characteristics of a capitalist economic system. A feminized culture is intimidated by individualism and competition and therefore finds the ideas of collectivism and communitarianism irresistible. The concept of individuals having to responsibly produce anything is rather intimidating to a culture that has lost its masculinity. That's why some of the terms used to sell socialism, communism, and Marxism are collectivism and communitarianism. It all sounds so cozy and fun, doesn't it?

Marxism presents a lie to the masses that wealth is static, although if you study Marx's writings, you see that he didn't really believe that. The message is that people fight and compete for this finite bucket of wealth in the world. Marxism treats economics as a simple Easter egg hunt, where at the end of the hunt, half of the players who find a less-than-average amount of Easter eggs are classified as a victim group.

The Marxist economic message to the "workers" is always something like, "Rise up, seize the means of production, then you can write your own paycheck!" There are a host of horrible problems with anyone seizing means of production that do not belong to them. The first is that it's stealing. The second is that those means of production effectively compete with other means of production (other factories, for example). This limits the ability of the "worker" to increase his or her paycheck. The third problem is that assembly line workers are not experts at maintaining means of production. In practice, "workers seizing means of production" is as destructive as the Allied bombing of German factories in World War II. There are a few more things that Marxists don't tell you. One is that "workers" (I put quotes on that because pretty much everyone works) don't share in the losses if the company or idea fails. The other is that in the United States, many employees at lower levels on the organizational structure own stock in the companies they work for.

The Switch

In one of the most successful propaganda campaigns in history, Marxists have convinced people that the cure for oppression is more oppression. Marxism is often presented as being altruistic and "Christian" because of its ostensible goal to help the poor. But the overall ability of an economy is hindered from creating wealth in a Marxist economy. Historically, millions of people have been executed or starved to death under Marxism.

The moral track record of Marxism suggests that a Marxist government would have a unique advantage over capitalism in eliminating poverty because the Marxist government could simply murder all the poor people. No kidding, that's the type of option that is on the table with purely Marxist regimes.

There are four lies that Marx promotes in his war on property rights. Here is a summary:[19]

1) A person's identity is defined by their work.
2) The institution of property rights is portrayed as an "original sin."
3) Workers under capitalism are "alienated" because of the division of labor.
4) Redemption is obtained through the abolition of private property.

---

[19] https://tifwe.org/the-four-twisted-truths-of-marx/.

Never forget that genocide comes from a power differential coupled with an immoral authority. There is no moral cleansing power of centralizing means of production and eliminating private property. In fact, the opposite is likely to occur because "absolute power corrupts absolutely." How is another person's wealth hurting you? Wealth in another person's hands only hurts you if they are an immoral person. If they are a moral person, that wealth might be used to help you.

You will most likely be lied to, but here are some questions you need to ask any Antifa activist you should happen to meet: What do you want to do with that power you want? Why should we trust you? Does your "oppressed minority" status make you a more moral person?

At the time of his death in 2018, the Marxist dictator of Cuba, Fidel Castro, was estimated to have a net worth in the range of $900 million to $1 billion. Meanwhile, the common people of Cuba were barely surviving due to extreme poverty.

There are some other areas where Marxism fails miserably. Since people in a Marxist economy have no incentives to take risk, there is typically zero innovation with Marxism. The list of lifesaving inventions invented by Marxists is short. I can think of a certain type of eye surgery that was invented in the USSR because they were able to force political prisoners to submit to experimental surgery.

Here is the basic road map of the typical Marxist takeover of a nation:

1) Create conflict between the "haves" versus the "have nots."
2) Launch a revolution in order to centralize power.
3) Use that centralized power to oppress Christians, capitalists, and anyone else who values freedom.

Always look at Marxism "backward." Marxists have an endgame of oppressing Christians with totalitarian control. Then they push incremental "baby steps" to get there. If you can control a person's money, you have a better chance of controlling their religion. The "official" religion of Marxism is atheism. This is a lie. Like most atheists, Marxists are God-haters.

The Bible tells you that Marxism is destined to under-deliver, at best, in Mark 14:7.

> For you always have the poor with you, and whenever you want, you can do good to them; but you do not always have Me.

Egalitarianism
Chasing the Mirage of "Equality"

It has become an almost universal crusade to promote egalitarianism. Egalitarianism is defined by Merriam Webster as "1) a belief in human equality especially with respect to social, political, and economic affairs, 2) a social philosophy advocating the removal of inequalities among people."

Zachary Garris writes in *Masculine Christianity* that "egalitarians despise authority and therefore scorn hierarchy. They begin by rejecting God's authority, and they, in turn, reject Biblical authority structures."[20]

Egalitarians have done a good job of making several words pejoratives. "Power" is one. "Patriarchy" is another. On the other end of the spectrum, words like "anti-racist" go far beyond just being anti-racist. A good anti-racist is supposed to despise all perceived hierarchies, even to the point of promoting the LGBTQ agenda.

The first time we see "equality" advocated is in the Garden of Eden.

> Now the serpent was more cunning than any animal of the field which the Lord God had made. And he said to the woman, "Has God really said, 'You shall not eat from any tree of the garden?'" The woman said to the serpent, "From the fruit

---

[20] Zachary M. Garris, *Masculine Christianity* (Ann Arbor, MI: Zion Press, 2020), 8.

> of the trees of the garden we may eat; but from
> the fruit of the tree which is in the middle of the
> garden, God has said, 'You shall not eat from it
> or touch it, or you will die.'" The serpent said to
> the woman, "You certainly will not die! For God
> knows that on the day you eat from it your eyes
> will be opened, and you will become like God,
> knowing good and evil." (Genesis 3:1–5)

Note what Satan said in Genesis 3:5 that "gods" are presented as
the "haves" and Adam and Eve as the "have-nots." Satan was trying
to destroy the existing order by advocating "equality." Be leery of
anyone who says, "It's not fair!" then advocates sin and destruction
as the way to set everything right. "It's wrong!" or "It's right" is more
important than "It's not fair!" Life is not fair.

A key lie that egalitarians, cultural Marxists, and "Social Justice
warriors" advocate is that God is egalitarian. This is simply not true.
Liberal theologians struggle mightily to get any ideas that God is
egalitarian past the first chapters of Genesis, but there is more.

Moving ahead to Exodus 20, we can see the foundation of biblical civil government, which is the Ten Commandments:

> Then God spoke all these words, saying, "I am
> the Lord your God, who brought you out of the
> land of Egypt, out of the house of slavery. You
> shall have no other gods before Me. You shall not
> make for yourself an idol, or any likeness of what
> is in heaven above or on the earth beneath or in
> the water under the earth. You shall not worship
> them or serve them; for I, the Lord your God, am
> a jealous God, visiting the iniquity of the fathers
> on the children, on the third and the fourth gen-
> erations of those who hate Me, but showing lov-
> ingkindness to thousands, to those who love Me
> and keep My commandments. You shall not take

the name of the Lord your God in vain, for the Lord will not leave him unpunished who takes His name in vain. Remember the sabbath day, to keep it holy. Six days you shall labor and do all your work, but the seventh day is a sabbath of the Lord your God; in it you shall not do any work, you or your son or your daughter, your male or your female servant or your cattle or your sojourner who stays with you. For in six days the Lord made the heavens and the earth, the sea and all that is in them, and rested on the seventh day; therefore the Lord blessed the sabbath day and made it holy. Honor your father and your mother, that your days may be prolonged in the land which the Lord your God gives you. You shall not murder. You shall not commit adultery. You shall not steal. You shall not bear false witness against your neighbor. You shall not covet your neighbor's house; you shall not covet your neighbor's wife or his male servant or his female servant or his ox or his donkey or anything that belongs to your neighbor."

Here are some general observations about the Ten Commandments:

1) There is a hierarchy between the lawgiver (God) and the law-receiver (mankind).
2) There is a hierarchy with God transcendent to all other gods (verses 3 and 4).
3) There is a hierarchy of parents over children (verse 12).
4) God is pro-life (verse 13).
5) God endorsed private property (verse 15).
6) There is a demarcation between truth and lies (verse 16).
7) We are not even to covet another person's property.

8) The law is bottom-up.
9) The Ten Commandments are given to individuals, not groups.

Here is a question to ponder: Were hierarchies created, or did they evolve? This is one of those irritating binary questions. There are two possible answers:

1) Hierarchies evolved. If hierarchies evolved, what moral authority does anyone have to question the process of evolution, especially if you believed you evolved from it?
2) Hierarchies were created. If hierarchies were created, then who created them? If you believe God created them, did he make a mistake? If someone else created them, who was it?

One would expect egalitarians to be anarchists, but they need the state's power to dismantle current hierarchies. The main take-away here is that the endgame of egalitarianism is to dismantle the existing hierarchies, not create equality. It is absolutely impossible to make everyone equal in every way.

What about "Successful" Socialism?

Merriam Webster defines socialism as "any of various economic and political theories advocating collective or governmental ownership and administration of the means of production and distribution of goods." We commonly think of a socialistic government as one that has a mix of capitalism and state ownership and control of certain economic sectors, such as socialized medicine, for example. Karl Marx viewed socialism as the interim step between capitalism and Marxism. Historically, social-ism has been the "gateway drug" of Marxism, fascism, and any other form of totalitarianism. It's the initial step of a Hegelian compromise loop (we will discuss this in a future chapter) used to dismantle a capi-talistic economic system and implement centralized power.

The earliest warning about centralized power is recorded in the Bible. Here is 1 Samuel chapter 8:

> And it came about when Samuel was old that he appointed his sons judges over Israel. Now the name of his firstborn was Joel, and the name of his second, Abijah; they were judging in Beersheba. His sons, however, did not walk in his ways, but turned aside after dishonest gain and took bribes and perverted justice.
>
> Then all the elders of Israel gathered together and came to Samuel at Ramah; and they said to him, "Behold, you have grown old, and your sons do not walk in your ways. Now appoint a king for us to judge us like all the nations."
>
> But the thing was displeasing in the sight of Samuel when they said, "Give us a king to judge us." And Samuel prayed to the Lord. The Lord said to Samuel, "Listen to the voice of the people in regard to all that they say to you, for they have not rejected you, but they have rejected Me from being king over them. Like all the deeds which they have done since the day that I brought them up from Egypt even to this day—in that they have forsaken Me and served other gods— so they are doing to you also. Now then, listen to their voice; however, you shall solemnly warn them and tell them of the procedure of the king who will reign over them."
>
> So Samuel spoke all the words of the Lord to the people who had asked of him a king. He said, "This will be the procedure of the king who will

reign over you: he will take your sons and place them for himself in his chariots and among his horsemen and they will run before his chariots. He will appoint for himself commanders of thousands and of fifties, and some to do his plowing and to reap his harvest and to make his weapons of war and equipment for his chariots. He will also take your daughters for perfumers and cooks and bakers. He will take the best of your fields and your vineyards and your olive groves and give them to his servants. He will take a tenth of your seed and of your vineyards and give to his officers and to his servants. He will also take your male servants and your female servants and your best young men and your donkeys and use them for his work. He will take a tenth of your flocks, and you yourselves will become his servants. Then you will cry out in that day because of your king whom you have chosen for yourselves, but the Lord will not answer you in that day."

Nevertheless, the people refused to listen to the voice of Samuel, and they said, "No, but there shall be a king over us, that we also may be like all the nations, that our king may judge us and go out before us and fight our battles."

Now after Samuel had heard all the words of the people, he repeated them in the Lord's hearing. The Lord said to Samuel, "Listen to their voice and appoint them a king."

So Samuel said to the men of Israel, "Go every man to his city."

The United States was birthed as an escape from tyranny, just like nations at the Tower of Babel were birthed from globalism. The best-documented example in history of a king who was a tyrannical dictator is in the United States Declaration of Independence. Here is an excerpt referring to King George III of England:

> He has refused his assent to laws the most wholesome and necessary for the public good.
>
> He has forbidden his governors to pass laws of immediate and pressing importance, unless suspended in their operation till his assent should be obtained; and when so suspended, he has utterly neglected to attend to them.
>
> He has refused to pass other laws for the accommodation of large districts of people, unless those people would relinquish the right of representation in the legislature; a right inestimable to them and formidable to tyrants only.
>
> He has called together legislative bodies at places unusual, uncomfortable, and distant from the depository of their public records, for the sole purpose of fatiguing them into compliance with his measures.
>
> He has dissolved representative houses repeatedly, for opposing, with manly firmness, his invasions on the rights of the people.
>
> He has refused for a long time, after such dissolutions, to cause others to be elected; whereby the legislative powers, incapable of annihilation, have returned to the people at large for their exercise;

the state remaining in the meantime exposed to all the dangers of invasion from without, and convulsions within.

He has endeavored to prevent the population of these states; for that purpose obstructing the laws for naturalization of foreigners; refusing to pass others to encourage their migrations hither, and raising the conditions of new appropriations of lands.

He has obstructed the administration of justice, by refusing his assent to laws for establishing judiciary powers.

He has made judges dependent on his will alone, for the tenure of their offices, and the amount and payment of their salaries.

He has erected a multitude of new offices, and sent hither swarms of officers to harass our people, and eat out their substance.

He has kept among us, in times of peace, standing armies, without the consent of our legislatures.

He has affected to render the military independent of and superior to the civil power.

He has combined with others to subject us to a jurisdiction foreign to our constitution, and unacknowledged by our laws; giving his assent to their acts of pretended legislation:

- For quartering large bodies of armed troops among us;
- For protecting them, by a mock trial, from punishment for any murders which they should commit on the inhabitants of these states;
- For cutting off our trade with all parts of the world;
- For imposing taxes on us without our consent;
- For depriving us, in many cases, of the benefits of trial by jury;
- For transporting us beyond seas to be tried for pretended offenses;
- For abolishing the free system of English laws in a neighboring province, establishing therein an arbitrary government, and enlarging its boundaries, so as to render it at once an example and fit instrument for introducing the same absolute rule into these colonies;
- For taking away our charters, abolishing our most valuable laws, and altering fundamentally the forms of our governments;
- For suspending our own legislatures, and declaring themselves invested with power to legislate for us in all cases whatsoever.

He has abdicated government here, by declaring us out of his protection, and waging war against us.

He has plundered our seas, ravaged our coasts, burnt our towns, and destroyed the lives of our people.

He is at this time transporting large armies of foreign mercenaries to complete the works of death, desolation, and tyranny, already begun with circumstances of cruelty and perfidy scarcely paralleled in the most barbarous ages, and totally unworthy the head of a civilized nation.

He has constrained our fellow citizens, taken captive on the high seas, to bear arms against their country, to become the executioners of their friends and brethren, or to fall themselves by their hands.

He has excited domestic insurrections amongst us, and has endeavored to bring on the inhabitants of our frontiers, the merciless Indian savages, whose known rule of warfare is an undistinguished destruction of all ages, sexes, and conditions.

In every stage of these oppressions, we have petitioned for redress, in the most humble terms. Our repeated petitions have been answered only by repeated injury. A prince, whose character is thus marked by every act which may define a tyrant, is unfit to be the ruler of a free people.

King George ended up being the most valuable tyrant in world history because the governmental system of the United States was designed to limit the power of any future would-be King George.

The statement that "power corrupts, and absolute power corrupts absolutely" has proven to be true many times throughout history. The

United States government was structured to have a system of checks and balances to maximize the ability of people to govern themselves.

The Scandinavian countries are often held up as shining examples of successful socialism. But there is a lot more to that story.[21] Although Sweden and Denmark have extensive social programs, they are foundationally capitalist and free market.

I could bore you with a deep economic analysis, but the primary difference in economic systems between the Scandinavian countries and other countries I have found is that the national government of Norway actively buys stock in private companies. I am not sure if this is good or bad, but it sure is nationalistic!

Since the Marxists have switched to a cultural Marxist attack on the US, you don't hear as much about Scandinavia as being a socialist success story. Scandinavia has historically been close to 100% White and has no history of slavery. It simply cannot be claimed that the wealth in Scandinavia was created by an "oppressor" class oppressing anyone.

Technocracy
Rescuing Socialism

Communism and Marxism have historically failed economically. It has been said that the only place that Marxism works is on college campuses, places that are subsidized by capitalism. Since Marxism always overproduces what is not needed and underproduces what is needed, the proposed solutions of Marxists always fall under two categories—better data and better tools. This really means total surveillance (better data) and total control (better tools). The beast described in Revelations will probably be sold to the world as the surveillance and artificial intelligence system that will finally make Marxism work economically. Marxism has ironically succeeded very well at its true goal, which is to persecute Christians. This new push for surveillance and control will be sold as technocracy.

---

[21] Anthony B. Kim and Julia Howe, "Why Democratic Socialists Can't Legitimately Claim Sweden or Denmark as Success Stories," eBook, Heritage Foundation.

There are several issues with technocracy:

1) It displaces elected representatives.
2) The "technocrats" are usually put in place with no checks and balances.
3) Technocracy can allow decisions to be made at the maximum distance from the actual problem.
4) The methodology to put the technocrats in power can be flawed.
5) The methodology to put the technocrats in power can be manipulated.
6) Technocracy implies that the morality of civil authority is irrelevant.
7) Technocracy implies that intellectual ability is far more important than morality.
8) Technocracy gives people moral authority based on their perceived intellectual ability.

Technology without morality is exactly what led to the construction and use of the Nazi gas chambers. Technocracy is disguised totalitarianism, but since it is allegedly based on intellectual ability, a lot of intellectual leaders are already trying to move everyone to the totalitarian technocracy. People such as Mark Zuckerberg, Bill Gates, etc., invest a lot of time in trying to manipulate the culture. It is evident that many Christian leaders have been deceived into working for the future totalitarian technocracy. These Christian leaders probably had their own egos used against them, and they were told that they would be a part of the moral "thought leadership" in the future order.

In order to sell technocracy, the beast needs to be fed large, difficult problems that are supposedly too large for any one person, family, or nation to solve. Here are some candidates:

1) Climate change (formerly known as global warming)
2) Global pandemic: notice how the governmental reaction to COVID-19 is far stronger than the threat itself.
3) World war: this is how the League of Nations was "sold" to the public after World War I, and the United Nations was "sold" to the public after World War II. It makes one wonder about the purpose of those wars.
4) Global inequality: this is where things dovetail very well with Marxism.
5) Financial crises: the inherently flawed fiat money system will start to unravel worldwide. Instead of going back to a gold or silver standard, another surprisingly honest money system, cryptocurrencies, will most likely be hijacked by central bankers to become the mark of the beast money system described in Revelations.

This short cartoon explains the Achilles heel of technocracy very well:

Perhaps the most dangerous aspect of technocracy is that it assumes that it is far more important to be smart than it is to be moral.

John Lennon and the Utopian Vision

One would expect that any push to the upper left quadrant (feminine totalitarianism) of the Political Identity Matrix would encounter mass resistance, especially from the more educated. I am not defending the upper right quadrant (masculine totalitarianism), but there is more data on how these Marxist/Communist systems have failed. The only thing they have not failed at is oppressing people. Someone is selling a lot of influential people on moving to the upper left. The process to promote this move is multifaceted.

In 1971 John Lennon released his highest-selling solo single called "Imagine." Here are the lyrics:

> Imagine there's no heaven
> It's easy if you try
> No hell below us
> Above us only sky
> Imagine all the people
> Living for today
>
> Imagine there's no countries
> It isn't hard to do
> Nothing to kill or die for
> And no religion too
> Imagine all the people
> Living life in peace
>
> You may say I'm a dreamer
> But I'm not the only one
> I hope someday you'll join us
> And the world will be as one

Imagine no possessions
I wonder if you can
No need for greed or hunger
A brotherhood of man
Imagine all the people
Sharing all the world

You may say I'm a dreamer
But I'm not the only one
I hope someday you'll join us
And the world will live as one

The tune for the song is slow and peaceful. The message of the song is that in building a utopia, several God-given boundaries need to be erased:

1) Heaven and hell, well, it seems like he wants to "imagine" away both hell and heaven.
2) Country borders must be abolished.
3) Religion must be abolished.
4) Private property must be abolished.

Lennon also says, "Above us only sky," and advocates "living for today," which would imply atheism. The utopia promises that "the world will live as one."

When shown on the Political Identity Matrix, John Lennon is describing a straight left move:

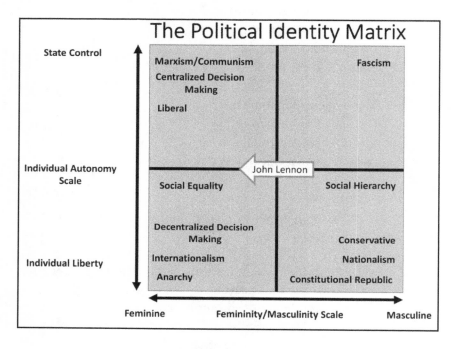

Lennon's song is a perfect example of the satanic deception used to sell the one-world government. The alleged utopia he sings about will be anything but.

Biblical Law Compared to Sharia Law

Geert Wilder, who is the Chairman of the Netherlands Party for Freedom and is a supporter of Israel, in *warning about Islam,* makes an assessment that many accept, "Let no one fool you about Islam being a religion. Sure, it has a god and a hereafter and seventy-two virgins. But in its essence, Islam is a political ideology. It is a system that lays down detailed rules for society and the life of every person. Islam wants to dictate every aspect of life. Islam means 'submission.' Islam is not compatible with freedom and democracy because what it strives for is sharia. If you want to compare Islam to anything, compare it to communism or national socialism. These are all totalitarian ideologies."[22]

The main takeaway is that biblical law is "bottom-up" while Sharia law is "top-down." In a world that is becoming increasingly lawless, any law has a certain appeal. You need to know the difference between the two major systems of law. Sharia is the template that is used by Islam to impose a top-down control system on another country. Americans are often preached to "respect the local culture." Sharia is utilized to destroy the local culture of another country.

Globalism

Globalism is the attitude or policy of placing the interests of the entire world above those of individual nations.[23] Globalism is working toward establishing a system that is being pushed, sold, and hyper-marketed as a future nirvana on earth where strife becomes obsolete due to the erasure of national borders and the elimination of cultural and religious differences. The purpose of this article is to show you that the globalistic future state and all its interim steps are actually parts of the most evil and intolerant religion in the history of the world.

The Bible prophesies this future religious system. The most detailed description is in Revelation 13 that we read earlier.

Here is a summary of the prophecy in Revelation 13:

1) There will be a one-world religion.
2) There will be a one-world government.
3) There will be a one-world economic system.
4) Anyone who does not worship the image of the beast will receive the death penalty.
5) Anyone who does not join the economic system will not be allowed to buy or sell.

---

[22] Robert Pickle, "Sharia and Talmudic Law not Compatible with Christianity," August 9, 2016, https://noahidenews.com/2016/08/09/sharia-and-talmudic-law-not-compatible-with-christianity/.
[23] Dictionary.com.

Because this religion/government/economic system will rule the entire world, nobody will be able to opt out. It will be a top-down dictatorship. The system is obviously the most evil, oppressive, and intolerant regime the world will have ever known.

But let's say you are an atheist. Or let's say you, for one reason or another, do not believe the Bible or at least this interpretation of the Bible. I challenge you to study recorded history and find one case where centralization made life better for the common person. The structure of the United States government was a radical experiment in decentralization, limited authority, and checks and balances. This decentralized governmental system produced the most prosperous and successful nation in the history of the world.

On the other hand, even if a benevolent ruler is found to rule the world, you are only a regime change away from a Hitler or a Stalin. George Orwell provides an amazing extrapolation of the dangers of globalism in his classic novel 1984. In 1984, you can see where an abusive totalitarian government can end up without checks and balances—thought police, total surveillance, historical revisionism, total censorship, perpetual war, opposition defined as "insanity" that must be "cured," and the superstate. Sir John Dalberg-Acton said, "Power tends to corrupt. Absolute power corrupts absolutely." One of the early lessons from the founding of this country is that the greater the distance between the ruled and the ruler, the greater the likelihood of abusive, tyrannical rule. If you do a word analysis on the Declaration of Independence, you will see that the most common theme is complaints against the king of England for mistreating the colonists. Globalism wants to completely reverse the Declaration of Independence and restore the opportunity for mistreatment by a tyrannical power.

Today, if you dare oppose the globalist agenda, you are treated as either extremely ignorant or extremely evil. They think you are ruining their big chance at utopia. Globalists point to things like "free trade" as being universally good in all situations. "Free trade" has actually been "unfair trade" and has been a good deal for every country except the United States. US jobs have been offshored to countries that have lenient environmental and labor standards. It is a foundational economic principle that it is always more beneficial for a country to export than to import. When a country imports more than it exports, it causes a net outflow of wealth since the profit in every transaction belongs to the seller. But this imbalance is by design. The globalists know that in order to create their "New World Order," the United States must be weakened economically in order to provide a reason for the change.

Once you know the globalist endgame, you can predict the interim steps: massive immigration, erasure of national borders, a weakening of all religious beliefs, and combining currencies.

Globalism seems to have near-total control over the world's "thought leadership," which makes it seem as though anyone who opposes it is a "narrow-minded" deviant who is completely out of mainstream intellectual thought. The reason for this phenomenon is that one of the first groups of institutions that were taken over by globalistic influence was the world's central banks. These banks pretend to be public but are actually private and have zero public audit control. That means that they can secretly create money and fund almost any politician, cause, media company, or enterprise that they desire. No official mechanism is in place to even detect this type of transaction. That is why any efforts to audit the United States Federal Reserve (it is neither federal nor a reserve) have been resisted and overcome by the globalists.

Because globalists believe that their ultra-righteous ends justify ultra-evil means, things like pandemics and terrorism are secretly valued by the globalists. They need many diseases and conflicts so they can offer their globalistic cures.

So hopefully, I have "connected the dots" to show you the globalistic path that the world has been on for decades. Globalism strives to construct the most evil and intolerant religion in the history of the world. The fight against globalism must be multifaceted since the promotion and imposition of globalism are multifaceted as well.

CHAPTER 5

The War on Masculine Men— Satan's Force Multiplier

A force multiplier is a strategy or situation that enables the leveraging of an applied force. The old adage "Kill two birds with one stone" describes a force multiplier. We will now look at a crucial force multiplier that is having a huge impact on our nation, our churches, our families, and ourselves.

Masculine Patriarchy
The Common Thread

The biggest revelation to me when researching for this book is that the common thread between personal identity and political identity is the degree of masculinity in the Personal Identity Matrix and the degree of patriarchy in the Political Identity Matrix. It became evident to me that when God engineered this world, it was foundational in His design that men act like men and women act like women. If you look at the Personal Identity Matrix and the Political Identity Matrix next to each other, you will see how intricately linked the sexual identity components are. Because we have strayed from the intended design, the lack of masculine patriarchy is wreaking havoc on our culture. For example, there are pastors who know the truth but are getting ideologically bullied into compromising their beliefs.

Let's look at the Personal Identity Matrix and the Political Identity Matrix together. The Political Identity Matrix is on the top. The Personal Identity Matrix is on the bottom.

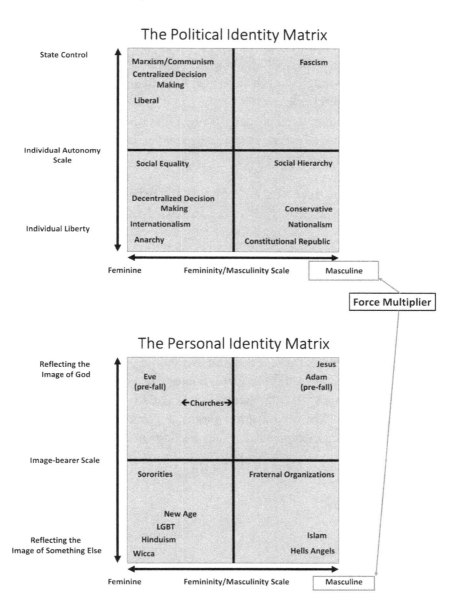

Because the masculine/feminine dynamic is on both matrices, Satan and his followers can use the powerful force multiplier of neutralizing masculine men to achieve their goals. We have gone from the crossfire at the beginning of the book where Christian men were attacked not only for their Christianity but also their masculinity, to seeing the additional leverage on the Political Identity Matrix of attacking men and masculinity. In order to explore how Satan and his followers operate on both matrices, we will start at the endgame and work our way back.

Patriarchy has been turned into a pejorative, but throughout the Bible and world history, it is usually the patriarchs who risk their lives to intercede for their people.

Interaction of the Political Identity Matrix with the Political Identity Matrix

Some of the political cop-outs you will hear from many people, especially modern or progressive pastors, is that "I stay out of politics" or "Democrats and Republicans are two wings of the same bird" or "You can be a Christian, and it doesn't matter if you are a liberal or conservative," etc. The motives for these statements are usually ignorance, cowardice, or a mix of the two. The reason these cop-out statements are suspicious is that each and every type of political structure is going to try to legislate, mandate, and create a certain type of citizen. For someone who calls themselves a Christian to either actively or tacitly promote a Sharia government, for example, is ridiculous at best. Let's take a deeper dive to see the logical disconnect in these cop-outs.

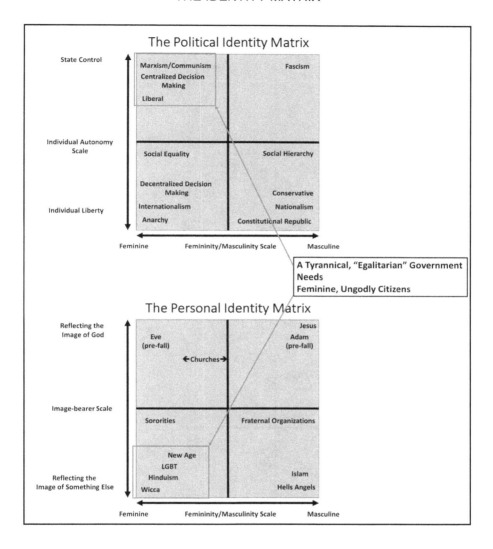

The chart above shows the interaction between the Political Identity Matrix and the Personal Identity Matrix. A tyrannical, "egalitarian" government needs feminine, ungodly citizens.

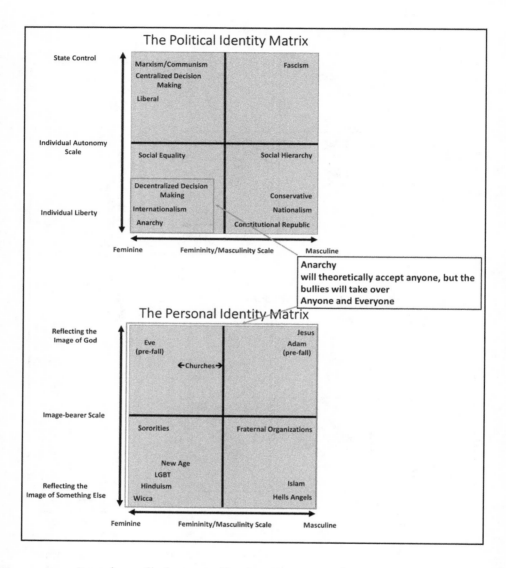

Anarchy will theoretically accept anyone, but the bullies will eventually take over.

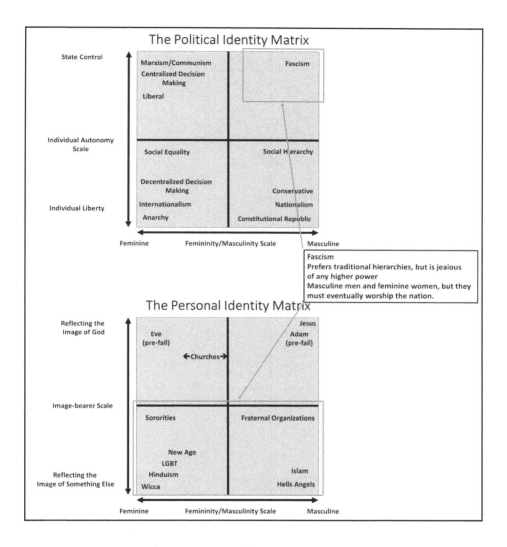

Fascism prefers traditional hierarchies but is jealous of any higher power. Masculine men and feminine men are usually desired by fascism, but they must eventually worship the nation.

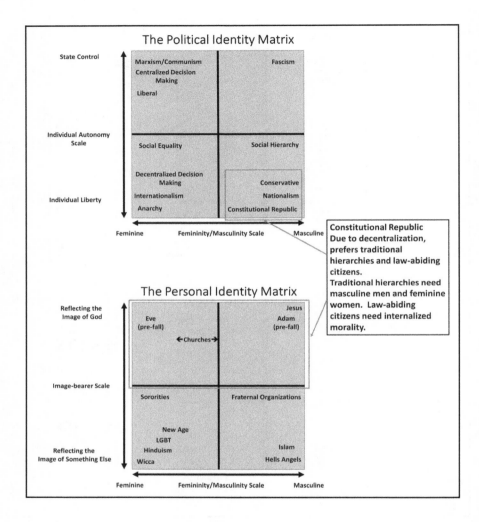

A Constitutional Republic prefers traditional hierarchies and law-abiding citizens. Traditional hierarchies need masculine men and feminine women. Law-abiding citizens need internalized morality.

The analysis above shows that it is impossible to truly be both a religious leader and a political agnostic. Any religious leader who claims to be politically agnostic is lying to you. Either they are conflict-phobes who are too cowardly to tell you, or they have a hidden agenda.

The Male Self-Identity of God

Zach Garris says in *Masculine Christianity*, "God always reveals Himself in masculine terms."[24] Any honest study of the Bible will show that God self-identifies as male. God reveals Himself to the world through His son Jesus. Jesus modeled the Lord's Prayer for us, "Our Father who art in heaven…" The latest error that some modern churches have started teaching is that the Holy Spirit has a predominantly feminine nature. This is simply not true. John C. P. Smith writes in Answers in Depth:

> First, it is noted that the word for spirit in Hebrew and Aramaic, רוּחַ (rûaḥ), functions grammatically most often as a feminine noun. This has led some to suggest that the Holy Spirit represents a feminine side of God. However, the word (rûaḥ) sometimes behaves as a masculine noun, a tendency that is particularly noticeable when the word occurs as part of the phrase, רוּחַ יהוה (Rûaḥ YHWH), "the Spirit of YHWH." The argument for femininity is further weakened by the fact that the equivalent Greek term, πνεῦμα (pneúma), is neuter (i.e., genderless). The Bible teaches that the Spirit of God proceeds from the (male) Father (John 15:26), and from the (male) Son (John 20:22), operating in and through both. Jesus, the man, was full of the Holy Spirit (Luke 4:1)—that did not make him female, or even half male and half female. The Holy Spirit is the Spirit of a God, who, as we have already

---

[24] Zachary M. Garris, *Masculine Christianity* (Ann Arbor, MI: Zion Press, 2020), 78.

noted, is consistently presented throughout the Scriptures as being male.[25]

There are a group of people who have an extreme emotional problem with God self-identifying as male. These people are called feminists, and their foundational belief is feminism. They can be female or male. The male pastor of your church may be a feminist. I will spare you the Greek and Hebrew analysis and take a deeper look at feminism. Now that you know the deeper motives of feminism, you will see the motives in everything they do.

Feminism

Feminism is a "sacred cow." Once someone declares themselves to be a feminist, they are typically categorized as a righteous crusader who can do no wrong. Feminists are great marketers. They have somehow convinced millions of women around the world that a woman's place is in the cubicle.

The first thing you notice about feminists is that most feminists are not feminine. My personal definition of a feminist is a person who resents the fact that God self-identifies as male. When you understand this, you quickly see that no amount of "equality" efforts will ever satisfy a feminist. That's because the true goal is not "equality." It's to attack God due to their resentment of His maleness, masculinity, and authority. Since the feminists are unable to find God to attack Him, they decide to attack the closest thing to God they can find. Usually, it's a Christian, an image-bearer.

As we saw earlier, God has self-identified as a straight male. Feminists will always have a problem with the maleness of God. Feminists will also have a problem with the authority of God. The LGBTQ will always have a problem with the "straightness" of God. No matter how much straight males, our culture, our government, or our churches give to these groups, they will never be happy. All the

[25] John C. P. Smith, "Does God Have a Gender?" June 3, 2020, https://answersingenesis.org/who-is-god/does-god-have-gender/.

equality efforts in the world will not make certain people happy. It's not about equality. It's about resentment. This is why the feminists are not upset at transgender athletes taking trophies from women. Is it about helping women or hurting men?

Jezebel

In order to fully understand the spirit of feminism, you need to know the biblical story of Jezebel. I consider Jezebel to be the first feminist. And if you think I am making a harsh exaggeration, keep in mind that that one of the leading feminist websites is named jezebel.com. Most historical knowledge of Jezebel comes straight from the Bible. Here are the passages that describe her.

We first see Jezebel in 1 Kings 16:31:

> It came about, as though it had been a trivial thing for him to walk in the sins of Jeroboam the son of Nebat, that he married Jezebel the daughter of Ethbaal king of the Sidonians, and went to serve Baal and worshiped him.
>
> Now it happened after many days that the word of the Lord came to Elijah in the third year, saying, "Go, show yourself to Ahab, and I will send rain on the face of the earth." So Elijah went to show himself to Ahab. Now the famine was severe in Samaria. Ahab called Obadiah who was over the household. (Now Obadiah feared the Lord greatly; for when Jezebel destroyed the prophets of the Lord, Obadiah took a hundred prophets and hid them by fifties in a cave, and provided them with bread and water.) Then Ahab said to Obadiah, "Go through the land to all the springs of water and to all the valleys; perhaps we will find grass and keep the horses and mules alive, and not have to kill some of the cattle." So

they divided the land between them to survey it; Ahab went one way by himself and Obadiah went another way by himself. Now as Obadiah was on the way, behold, Elijah met him, and he recognized him and fell on his face and said, "Is this you, Elijah my master?" He said to him, "It is I. Go, say to your master, 'Behold, Elijah is here.'" He said, "What sin have I committed, that you are giving your servant into the hand of Ahab to put me to death? As the Lord your God lives, there is no nation or kingdom where my master has not sent to search for you; and when they said, 'He is not here,' he made the kingdom or nation swear that they could not find you. And now you are saying, 'Go, say to your master, "Behold, Elijah is here!"' It will come about when I leave you that the Spirit of the Lord will carry you where I do not know; so when I come and tell Ahab and he cannot find you, he will kill me, although I your servant have feared the Lord from my youth. Has it not been told to my master what I did when Jezebel killed the prophets of the Lord, that I hid a hundred prophets of the Lord by fifties in a cave, and provided them with bread and water? And now you are saying, 'Go, say to your master, "Behold, Elijah is here"'; he will then kill me." Elijah said, "As the Lord of hosts lives, before whom I stand, I will surely show myself to him today." So Obadiah went to meet Ahab and told him; and Ahab went to meet Elijah. When Ahab saw Elijah, Ahab said to him, "Is this you, you troubler of Israel?" He said, "I have not troubled Israel, but you and your father's house have, because you have forsaken the commandments of the Lord and you have followed the Baals. Now then send and gather to me all Israel at Mount Carmel, together with 450 prophets of Baal and 400 prophets of the Asherah, who eat at Jezebel's table." (I Kings 18:4)

Now Ahab told Jezebel all that Elijah had done, and how he had killed all the prophets with the sword. Then Jezebel sent a messenger to Elijah, saying, "So may the gods do to me and even more, if I do not make your life as the life of one of them by tomorrow about this time." (I Kings 19:1–2)

Now it came about after these things that Naboth the Jezreelite had a vineyard which was in Jezreel beside the palace of Ahab king of Samaria. Ahab spoke to Naboth, saying, "Give me your vineyard, that I may have it for a vegetable garden because it is close beside my house, and I will give you a better vineyard than it in its place; if you like, I will give you the price of it in money." But Naboth said to Ahab, "The Lord forbid me that I should give you the inheritance of my fathers." So Ahab came into his house sullen and vexed because of the word which Naboth the Jezreelite had spoken to him; for he said, "I will not give you the inheritance of my fathers." And he lay down on his bed and turned away his face and ate no food. But Jezebel his wife came to him and said to him, "How is it that your spirit is so sullen that you are not eating food?" So he said to her, "Because I spoke to Naboth the Jezreelite and said to him, 'Give me your vineyard for money; or else, if it pleases you, I will give you a vineyard in its place.' But he said, 'I will not give you my vineyard.'" Jezebel his wife said to him, "Do you now reign over Israel? Arise, eat bread, and let your heart be joyful; I will give you the vineyard of Naboth the Jezreelite." So she wrote letters in Ahab's name and sealed them with his seal, and sent letters to the elders and to the nobles who were living with Naboth in his city. Now she wrote in the letters, saying, "Proclaim a fast and seat Naboth at the head of the people; and seat two worthless men before him, and let them testify against him, saying, 'You cursed God and the king.' Then take him out and stone him to death." (I Kings 21:1–25)

Jezebel's Plot

So the men of his city, the elders and the nobles who lived in his city, did as Jezebel had sent word to them, just as it was written in the letters which she had sent them. They proclaimed a fast and seated Naboth at the head of the people. Then the two worthless men came in and sat before him; and the worthless men testified against him, even against Naboth, before the people, saying, "Naboth cursed God and the king." So they took him outside the city and stoned him to death with stones. Then they sent word to Jezebel, saying, "Naboth has been stoned and is dead." When Jezebel heard that Naboth had been stoned and was dead, Jezebel said to Ahab, "Arise, take possession of the vineyard of Naboth, the Jezreelite, which he refused to give you for money; for Naboth is not alive, but dead." When Ahab heard that Naboth was dead, Ahab arose to go down to the vineyard of Naboth the Jezreelite, to take possession of it. Then the word of the Lord came to Elijah the Tishbite, saying, "Arise, go down to meet Ahab king of Israel, who is in Samaria; behold, he is in the vineyard of Naboth where he has gone down to take possession of it. You shall speak to him, saying, 'Thus says the Lord, "Have you murdered and also taken possession?" And you shall speak to him, saying, 'Thus says the Lord, "In the place where the dogs licked up the blood of Naboth the dogs will lick up your blood, even yours."'" Ahab said to Elijah, "Have you found me, O my enemy?" And he answered, "I have found you, because you have sold yourself to do evil in the sight of the Lord. Behold, I will bring evil upon you, and will utterly sweep you away, and will cut off from Ahab every male, both bond and free in Israel; and I will make your house like the house of Jeroboam the son of Nebat, and like the house of Baasha the son of Ahijah, because of the provocation with which you have provoked Me to anger, and because you have made Israel sin. Of Jezebel also has the Lord spoken, saying, 'The dogs will eat Jezebel in the district of Jezreel.' The one belonging to Ahab, who dies in the city, the dogs will eat, and the one who dies in the field the birds of heaven will eat." Surely there was no one like Ahab who sold himself to do evil in the sight of the Lord, because Jezebel his wife incited him.

Now Elisha the prophet called one of the sons of the prophets and said to him, "Gird up your loins, and take this flask of oil in your hand and go to Ramoth-gilead. When you arrive there, search out Jehu the son of Jehoshaphat the son of

Nimshi, and go in and bid him arise from among his brothers, and bring him to an inner room. Then take the flask of oil and pour it on his head and say, 'Thus says the Lord, "I have anointed you king over Israel."' Then open the door and flee and do not wait." So the young man, the servant of the prophet, went to Ramoth-gilead. When he came, behold, the captains of the army were sitting, and he said, "I have a word for you, O captain." And Jehu said, "For which one of us?" And he said, "For you, O captain." He arose and went into the house, and he poured the oil on his head and said to him, "Thus says the Lord, the God of Israel, 'I have anointed you king over the people of the Lord, even over Israel. You shall strike the house of Ahab your master, that I may avenge the blood of My servants the prophets, and the blood of all the servants of the Lord, at the hand of Jezebel. For the whole house of Ahab shall perish, and I will cut off from Ahab every male person both bond and free in Israel. I will make the house of Ahab like the house of Jeroboam the son of Nebat, and like the house of Baasha the son of Ahijah. The dogs shall eat Jezebel in the territory of Jezreel, and none shall bury her.'" Then he opened the door and fled. Now Jehu came out to the servants of his master, and one said to him, "Is all well? Why did this mad fellow come to you?" And he said to them, "You know very well the man and his talk." They said, "It is a lie, tell us now." And he said, "Thus and thus he said to me, 'Thus says the Lord, "I have anointed you king over Israel."'" Then they hurried and each man took his garment and placed it under him on the bare steps, and blew the trumpet, saying, "Jehu is king!" (II Kings 9:1–37)

Jehoram (Joram) Is Assassinated

So Jehu the son of Jehoshaphat the son of Nimshi conspired against Joram. Now Joram with all Israel was defending Ramoth-gilead against Hazael king of Aram, but King Joram had returned to Jezreel to be healed of the wounds which the Arameans had inflicted on him when he fought with Hazael king of Aram. So Jehu said, "If this is your mind, then let no one escape or leave the city to go tell it in Jezreel." Then Jehu rode in a chariot and went to Jezreel, for Joram was lying there. Ahaziah king of Judah had come down to see Joram. Now the watchman was standing on the tower in Jezreel, and he saw the company of Jehu as he came, and said, "I see a company." And Joram said, "Take a horseman and send him to meet them and let him say, 'Is it peace?'" So a horseman went to meet him and said, "Thus says the king, 'Is it peace?'" And Jehu said, "What have you to do with peace? Turn behind me." And the watchman reported, "The messenger came to them, but he did not return." Then he sent out a second horseman, who came to them and said, "Thus says the king, 'Is it peace?'" And Jehu answered, "What have you to do with peace? Turn behind me." The watchman reported, "He came even to them, and he did not return; and the driving is like the driving of Jehu the son of Nimshi, for he drives furiously." Then Joram said, "Get ready." And they made his chariot ready. Joram king of Israel and Ahaziah king of Judah went out, each in his chariot, and they went out to meet Jehu and found him in the property of Naboth the Jezreelite. When Joram saw Jehu, he said, "Is it peace, Jehu?" And he answered, "What peace, so long as the harlotries of your mother Jezebel and her witchcrafts are so many?" So Joram reined about and fled and said to Ahaziah, "There is treachery, O Ahaziah!" And Jehu drew his bow with his full strength and shot Joram between his arms; and the arrow went through his heart and he sank in his chariot. Then Jehu said to Bidkar his officer, "Take him up and cast him into the property of the field of Naboth the Jezreelite, for I remember when you and I were riding together after Ahab his father, that the Lord laid this oracle against him: 'Surely, I have seen yesterday the blood of Naboth and the blood of his sons,' says the Lord, and 'I will repay you in this property,' says the Lord. Now then, take and cast him into the property, according to the word of the Lord."

Jehu Assassinates Ahaziah

When Ahaziah the king of Judah saw this, he fled by the way of the garden house. And Jehu pursued him and said, "Shoot him too, in the chariot." So they shot him at the ascent of Gur, which is at Ibleam. But he fled to Megiddo and died there. Then his servants carried him in a chariot to Jerusalem and buried him in his grave with his fathers in the city of David. Now in the eleventh year of Joram, the son of Ahab, Ahaziah became king over Judah. When Jehu came to Jezreel, Jezebel heard of it, and she painted her eyes and adorned her head and looked out the window. As Jehu entered the gate, she said, "Is it well, Zimri, your master's murderer?" Then he lifted up his face to the window and said, "Who is on my side? Who?" And two or three officials looked down at him.

Jezebel Is Slain

He said, "Throw her down." So they threw her down, and some of her blood was sprinkled on the wall and on the horses, and he trampled her under foot. When he came in, he ate and drank; and he said, "See now to this cursed woman and bury her, for she is a king's daughter." They went to bury her, but they found nothing more of her than the skull and the feet and the palms of her hands. Therefore they returned and told him. And he said, "This is the word of the Lord, which He spoke by His servant Elijah the Tishbite, saying, 'In the property of Jezreel the dogs shall eat the flesh of Jezebel; and the corpse of Jezebel will be as dung on the face of the field in the property of Jezreel, so they cannot say, "This is Jezebel."'"

Before we talk further about Jezebel, we need to delve deeper into Baal worship. The best summary of Baal and Asherah worship I have found is from thattheworldmayknow.com with Ray Vander Laan. His article is titled "Fertility Cults of Canaan."

Baal

The earliest deity recognized by the peoples of the ancient Near East was the creator god El. His mistress, the fertility goddess Asherah, gave birth to many gods, including a powerful god named

Baal (Lord). There appears to have been only one Baal, who was manifested in lesser Baals at different places and times. Over the years, Baal became the dominant deity, and the worship of El faded.

Baal won his dominance by defeating the other deities, including the god of the sea, the god of storms (also of rain, thunder, and lightning), and the god of death. Baal's victory over death was thought to be repeated each year when he returned from the land of death (underworld), bringing rain to renew the earth's fertility. Hebrew culture viewed the sea as evil and destructive, so Baal's promise to prevent storms and control the sea, as well as his ability to produce abundant harvests, made him attractive to the Israelites. It's hard to know why Yahweh's people failed to see that he alone had power over these things. Possibly, their desert origins led them to question God's sovereignty over fertile land. Or maybe it was simply the sinful pagan practices that attracted them to Baal.

Baal is portrayed as a man with the head and horns of a bull, an image similar to that in biblical accounts. His right hand (sometimes both hands) is raised, and he holds a lightning bolt, signifying both destruction and fertility. Baal has also been portrayed seated on a throne, possibly as the king or lord of the gods.

Asherah

Asherah was honored as the fertility goddess in various forms and with varying names (Judges 3:7). The Bible does not actually describe the goddess, but archaeologists have discovered figurines believed to be representations of her. She is portrayed as a nude female, sometimes pregnant, with exaggerated breasts that she holds out, apparently as symbols of the fertility she promises her followers. The Bible indicates that she was worshiped near trees and poles, called Asherah poles (Deuteronomy 7:5, 12:2–3, II Kings 16:4, 17:10, Jeremiah 3:6,13, Ezekiel 6:13).

Cultic Practices

Baal's worshipers appeased him by offering sacrifices, usually animals such as sheep or bulls (I Kings 18:23). Some scholars believe that the Canaanites also sacrificed pigs and that God prohibited his people from eating pork in part to prevent this horrible cult from being established among them. (See Isaiah 65:1–5 for an example of Israel's participating in the pagan practices of the Canaanites.) At times of crisis, Baal's followers sacrificed their children, apparently the firstborn of the community, to gain personal prosperity. The Bible called this practice "detestable" (Deuteronomy 12:31, 18:9–10). God specifically appointed the tribe of Levi as his special servants, in place of the firstborn of the Israelites, so they had no excuse for offering their children (Numbers 3:11–13). The Bible's repeated condemnation of child sacrifice shows God's hatred of it, especially among his people.

Asherah was worshiped in various ways, including through ritual sex. Although she was believed to be Baal's mother, she was also his mistress. Pagans practiced "sympathetic magic," that is, they believed they could influence the gods' actions by performing the behavior they wished the gods to demonstrate. Believing the sexual union of Baal and Asherah produced fertility, their worshipers engaged in immoral sex to cause the gods to join together, ensuring good harvests. This practice became the basis for religious prostitution (I Kings 14:23–24). The priest or a male member of the community represented Baal. The priestess or a female member of the community represented Asherah. In this way, God's incredible gift of sexuality was perverted to the most obscene public prostitution. No wonder God's anger burned against his people and their leaders.

Here are some things we can observe about Jezebel:

1) Jezebel "hijacked" a king (Ahab).
2) Jezebel was from Sidon, a seaport in what is now Lebanon.
3) Jezebel worshiped Baal.
4) Jezebel's father was Ethbaal, or Ithobaal, who was a priest of Astarte.
5) Astarte is the Hellenized form of the goddess Ashtoreth, a form of Ishtar (English form is Easter).
6) Ethobaal means "with Baal."
7) Jezebel not only worshiped Baal, but she also served him.
8) Jezebel liked to murder the prophets of Yahweh.
9) Jezebel dined with the prophets of Baal and Asherah.
10) Jezebel used power from King Ahab by forging his name and seal.
11) Jezebel was passive-aggressive.
12) Jezebel incited her husband to do evil.
13) Jezebel was guilty of harlotries and witchcraft.
14) Jezebel painted her eyes and adorned her head.
15) Jezebel made a veiled threat (Zimri).
16) Jezebel was a hypocrite.
17) Jezebel died a horrible death that fulfilled prophecy.

Some people may think that it is no longer relevant to study Jezebel. But Jezebel is mentioned in the New Testament, in Revelation 2:20–24.

> But I have this against you, that you tolerate the woman Jezebel, who calls herself a prophetess, and she teaches and leads My bond-servants astray so that they commit acts of immorality and eat things sacrificed to idols. I gave her time to repent, and she does not want to repent of her immorality. Behold, I will throw her on a bed of sickness, and those who commit adultery with her into great tribulation unless they repent of her deeds. And I will kill her children with pestilence, and all the churches will know that I am He who searches the minds and hearts; and I will give to each one of you according to your deeds. But I say to you, the rest who are in Thyatira, who do not hold this teaching, who have not known the deep things of Satan, as they call them-I place no other burden on you.

So what can we learn from Jezebel? There is still a strong cultural association between Jezebel and evil. The lesson that has been lost is that Jezebel was all about raw power. When evil is coupled with power, many people suffer, even to the point of death. When you evaluate what feminists are really after, you will see that the lust for power is probably the primary driver in that movement. You see the coupling of the lust for power with evil in the feminist fixation on legalized (and tacitly promoting) abortion.

The True Goals of Feminism

Historically, there have been three major "waves" of feminism in the west. Instead of analyzing the past, my intent is to extrapolate to the endgame of feminism. If you study feminism, you will see that there is a "feminist playbook" (like the Communist Manifesto) that feminists apply over and over again. Here is what it looks like:

1) Try to promote unhappiness in women. This is the big motivator for everything else. This is why the leading feminists (gasp! Is there a hierarchy in feminism?) are also the angriest. There are three sources of the agitation:

   a. General unthankfulness for everything that their family, country, church, spouse, etc. has given them
   b. Envy, usually toward men
   c. Resentment, usually aimed at men but just below the surface (it's really at God)

2) Promote the idea of oppression in women. This is another motivator for their activism. It can get crazy here:

   a. They will complain about the unfairness of men not being attracted to overweight women. Yes, really.
   b. They seem mad at God for gender (sex) differences, but most believe in evolution.
   c. They search for perceived inequalities. The "oppression porn" here can apply to the past or to the current situation in the culture.

3) Here is a list of many of their proposed solutions to the above:

   a. Promote abortion ostensibly to liberate women (not the unborn women) so they can have consequence-free sex
   b. Declare war on marriage
   c. Promote man-free families
   d. Hate men, but yet…

e.   Try to be like men (more masculine)
f.   Claim to want equality but really identicality
g.   Promote socialism ("equality" means equal failure for all)
h.   Divorce your husband
i.   Become a witch

   i.   Witchcraft has the feminine allure of secret knowledge (Gnosticism) that is first seen in Genesis 3:5.

      Satan said, "For God knows that in the day you eat from it your eyes will be opened, and you will be like God, knowing good and evil."

   ii.   Spellcasting is the ultimate passive aggression.

j.   Advocate intergenerational retribution for past "oppression" by men.
k.   Take money and power from men (those same men they claim to be superior to and therefore not need).

It is suspicious that there are some women's issues that feminists never care much about, such as the trafficking of women, transgender male athletes competing against (and absolutely dominating) women, or unborn females being aborted.

Nobody has degraded motherhood more than feminists. But historically, when war breaks out, whichever side has had the most babies will usually win in the long term. Notice that feminists never try to infiltrate and/or attack the Shriners, Masons, Antifa, human trafficking rings, or the Hells Angels. But they will infiltrate and/or attack your church. Feminists exist to destroy God-given hierarchies. That's the endgame.

The Feminism—Witchcraft Connection

If you can remember someone reading you nursery rhyme books and children's books, like *Hansel and Gretel*, you remember pictures of witches. They were almost always depicted as ugly and old. Since feminism is all about power, it is only natural that there is a strong connection between feminism and witchcraft. Witchcraft is often packaged with a "good" gateway such as healing or herbalism. This is why in Africa, the sorcerers are often called witch doctors. Witches have been attempting periodically to cast spells on Donald Trump ever since he was elected. They are not doing this for fun or as a joke. The witches have every intention of harming people to further their agenda.

In medieval art, images of babies were often used to portray angels. That's because babies are probably the best "image-bearers" of God since they are more innocent. This probably explains why supporting abortion is a litmus test or rite of passage for feminists. Due to the witchcraft connection, feminists hate image-bearers.

The War on Masculinity

Why could there be, or why would there be, any sort of war on masculinity? Before we get into actual evidence, let's look at possible motives and possible suspects. If you want to conquer something, would you rather it be feminine or masculine? It is a great strategy to attempt to influence whatever you're trying to conquer, whether it's a person or organization, to be more feminine. It would make it easier for you to destroy it. We can also use the Personal Identity Matrix to find what I will call good masculinity versus toxic masculinity. Toxic is the lower right. Good is the upper right. Satan has moved so many men to the lower right. Now he's going for the kill shot to move them to the lower left, which is to feminize them. You can sense an overall anti-men attitude in modern cultures that I'm convinced comes from Satan's jealousy and hatred of all of God's attributes. God the Father, Jesus, and the Holy Spirit are clearly masculine beings. God is first identified in the Bible in Genesis 1:16, "God made two great lights, the greater light to govern the day, and the lesser light to govern the night; He made the stars also." It's not surprising that Satan would have a bad attitude toward all things masculine.

Modern culture has decided that all masculinity is "toxic masculinity." It has also been decided that all evil is masculine. The propaganda war on men is so bad that if men aren't careful when they sit down, they can be accused of "manspreading." If they try to help someone understand something, they can be accused of "mansplaining."

As if the cultural war on masculinity were not enough, medical research has been monitoring in men worldwide a precipitous drop in both testosterone and sperm count for the last several decades.[26] Estrogen is almost free, thanks to subsidized birth control. Free birth control pills can be obtained from county health departments or Planned Parenthood. On the other hand, testosterone costs around $4 per milligram and is a controlled substance. In exacerbating the problem, plastics have been proven to release estrogen and estrogen-increasing chemicals into the environment and, eventually, into human bodies. Because of both excreted estrogen from birth control pills and the explosion of plastic products, the environment is now at an all-time high in estrogen. Without getting into too much medical detail, this increase in estrogen is now coming under suspicion for how it is affecting men.

I am not going to get into molecular biology, but everyone needs to be aware of this issue so you can at least try to minimize the environmental factors that are impacting the hormone levels of both men and women. Please see your medical provider if you have any specific health concerns regarding this issue.

The War on Men

So now that we have laid out the case for the motive and the plausibility of a cultural attack on masculinity, the logical next step

---

[26] Neil Howe, "You're Not the Man Your Father Was," October 2, 2017, https://www.forbes.com/sites/neilhowe/2017/10/02/youre-not-the-man-your-father-was/?sh=1afab9bf8b7f

would be a war on men in general and on masculine men in particular. Let's see if there is any evidence.

The first thing we are going to look at is the statistics on some key metrics. [27]

Table 7 shows a summary of key statistics that show that things relating to men and women are far from a state of "equity." The general population in the United States is slightly more female, 50.75% versus 49.25% for men. Combat deaths show a stark contrast between men and women, with 99.9% of combat deaths being men. Work deaths are similar at 94% of men. The obvious statistical differences in homicide, suicide, prison population, prison sentencing, and autism diagnoses are all conveniently left out of the feminist narrative about "equality." College scholarships are given to four times as many females as males. And not surprisingly, college enrollment is about 56% female to 44% male when you analyze current incoming classes.

Metric	Male	Female
General Population	49.25	50.75
Combat Deaths	99.90%	0.10%
Work Deaths	94%	6%
Homicide Victims	76%	24%
Suicides	75%	25%
Prison Population	93%	7%
Prison time (sentencing for the same crime)	63% more	-
Autism diagnoses	80%	20%
College Scholarships	-	4 times more money
College Enrollment	44%	56%
Homeless	62%	38%

Table 7. Statistics for key metrics, men versus women.

Table 8 below shows key differences in how men and women are treated by the family court system in a divorce. These metrics are almost totally controlled by the family court system, and an entire

[27] Cassie Jaye, *The Red Pill*, DVD, directed by Cassie Jaye, Nena Jaye, Anna Laclergue, New York: ProSiebenSat.1 Media2016.

book could be written about that topic. But here are the key metrics. After a divorce, 82% of the time, the woman is given custody of the children, and 18% of the time, the man is given custody. The counterpoint of this is that it's often stated that the reason for this is that men do not fight for custody of their children. However, in a divorce, most of the time, both spouses are under financial stress, and it costs a lot of money to fight. A lot of men simply didn't have the money to fight for custody of their children. So if neither party has the resources to "fight," you can clearly see the default result that the woman will most likely end up with custody. Next, let's look at that custodial parent. When you break down the custodial parent who is receiving child support, 53.4% of those custodial parents, if they are women, will receive child support. Only 28.8% of the custodial parents, if they are men, will receive child support. The average child support paid by men is $5,450. The average child support paid by women is $3,500. If the man happens to not be the high-wage earner, the man only receives alimony about 3% of the time, and a woman in the same situation will receive alimony 97% of the time. You will hear a lot about the pay gap between men and women. This typically occurs in jobs that women don't want to do because the job is physically demanding, risky, or otherwise unpleasant. Since divorced women are more likely to have custody of the children, they are simply not available to work as many hours as divorced men. So before we start chanting about equal pay for equal work, let's have a conversation about equal child custody.

Metric	Male	Female
Child Custody	17.8	82.2
Custodial Parent Received CS	28.8	53.4
Avg Annual Child Support Payments	$5,450	$3,500
Alimony-high wage earner	67	33
Alimony receiver	3	97

Table 8. Divorce-related statistics, men versus women.

On top of all that, after the divorce is over, churches and charity organizations tend to resource the divorced women far more than the divorced men. This is probably because the women have custody of the children. Many churches have substituted divorced mothers and their children for the "widows and orphans" of the New Testament. It doesn't occur to most people that the divorced men might be missing both their children and their money. Or, more importantly, that those children are missing their biological father, who is now forced to expend resources just to visit his children. I have studied the reasons for this reaction of churches to divorced spouses, and here is what I have come up with. There are a lot of what I will call lazy ideas in the church about divorce. Femininity tends to have this strange Teflon effect. In other words, people and organizations are not comfortable ever saying anything negative about women, to the point that it's an off-limits topic. I think part of that is just some instinct we have that if the moms are bad, our culture is in deeper trouble than if the dads are bad. So there is that "want-to-believe" effect kicking in. But most churches and charity organizations would probably be surprised to find out that most divorces are initiated by the woman, not the man.

In summary, feminist initiatives and messaging only apply to power centers and to participation in "fun stuff." And your local church is most likely complicit in helping feminists achieve their objectives.

The War on Marriage

Marriage is an institution that was established in the Garden of Eden. For centuries, marriage has been administered by the church or whatever religion that the husband and wife subscribe to. It is unfortunate that civil government is even in the marriage "business." It makes no sense in a country such as the United States, where there is a plurality of faiths, to not have marriage solely administered by the church or religion of the people being married. The current situation is that the church is involved sometimes in premarital counseling then fully involved in the "fun stuff" of the wedding ceremony and reception. From that point on, the married couple is generally exempt from church discipline. If there is any trouble within the marriage relationship, counseling is usually offered by the church, but without the church discipline required to force both husband and wife to attend. From that point, the married couple usually pursues divorce, which is completely administered by the civil government. So the church gets to do the "fun stuff" of the wedding, and the civil government does the "messy stuff" of the divorce. As we have seen earlier, the civil courts are extremely biased against men. Thousands of pastors tacitly approve of this horrible scenario that continues to decimate families, weaken men, and feminize their churches. In feminized churches, right and wrong are typically determined by "underdog points." That means that the church will usually knee-jerk side with the woman in a divorce. It's the "nice" thing to do! The men continue to leave churches, and the church becomes more feminized. It's a vicious cycle.

Since the civil government is heavily involved in the "marriage business," it makes marriage an easier target to destroy. It makes the noble-sounding goal of eliminating "marriage discrimination" an easier battle for the LGBTQ coalition since civil government marriage is not solely Christian. Saying "gay marriage" is like saying "Muslim Bar Mitzvah," but most civil authorities don't really view marriage as having any form of moral foundation worth defending.

The War on Guns

Guns are masculine. Without getting too crude here, guns have both a masculine shape and a masculine way of functioning. Guns are a force multiplier. Guns can be used for hunting, which is a self-reliant, masculine activity. Every gun is designed to be used by a single person, so guns are not a communitarian team sport. Guns can be used for self-defense. Guns can be used for family defense. Guns can be used for national defense. Guns can be used to resist tyranny. Guns are protected by the Second Amendment of the US Constitution. This basically completes the freak-out bingo card for the totalitarian/egalitarian "left." So the left has a deep-seated hatred of guns. Any feigned media concern about "assault rifles," "mass shootings," and public safety is purely that, feigned. It's the first step in a compromise process. Don't give an inch.

Luke 11:21 says, "When a strong man, fully armed, guards his own house, his possessions are secure."

Fatherless Families

The welfare system and child support payments have taken the place of the provision that a father is supposed to provide. In many cases, a 911 call has taken the place of the discipline that a father used to provide. Fatherless sons are joining street gangs to fill the void in their lives caused by not having a father nearby. Both the male and female children lose the model of mature masculinity when a father is not in the house. By the way, this is no accident. Linda Gordon, a well-known feminist, said, "The nuclear family must be destroyed... whatever its ultimate meaning, the breakup of families now is an objectively revolutionary process."[28] To add insult to injury, there are now well-funded activists who are promoting the lie that two-parent homes are racist.[29]

Bullying the Boy Scouts

Boy Scouts of America (BSA) was founded in 1910.

To revisit something we looked at earlier, Boy Scouts checked a lot of boxes for helping turn boys into men:

---

[28] Jennifer Polk, "The Diminishing Dad," June 15, 2019, https://amgreatness.com/2019/06/15/the-diminishing-dad/.

[29] "The Black Supremacist Democrats of 'Black Twitter' Should Discuss Two-Parent Homes," March 11, 2021, https://lovebreedsaccountability.com/2021/03/11/the-black-supremacist-democrats-of-black-twitter-should-discuss-2-parent-homes/.

Risk life for others	X
Physical struggle or hazing	X
Separation from society	X
Liminal period	
Initiation rite	X
Given new powers or religion	X
Existence of heroes	
New name given (identity)	
New clothes given	X
Must pass a series of tests	X
Given new set of rules	X
Given new rights and privileges	X
Social bonding	X

Table 9. How the Boy Scouts of America turn boys into men.

On the Personal Identity Matrix, this is the vector on which the Boy Scouts were motivating the boys:

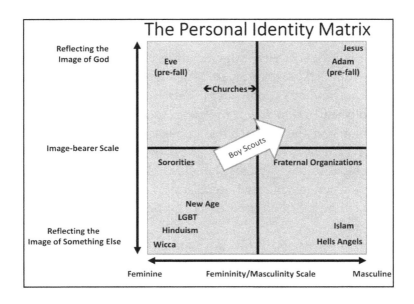

Without being involved in any political activities, this is what BSA was working to influence the boys' belief systems on the Political Identity Matrix:

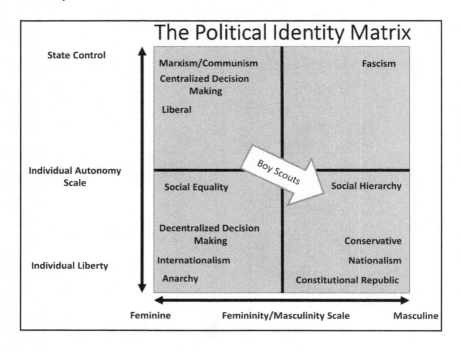

The Boy Scouts were targeted almost as soon as the organization was founded. According to Paul Kengor, "Exhibit 1 takes us way back to June 1911, only a year after the Boy Scouts of America was established. It's an article by Celia Rosatstein titled 'Why Boys Should Not Join the Boy Scouts,' published in the *Young Socialists'* Magazine. The article portrayed the Boy Scouts as gun-hungry, pro-war, bloodthirsty capitalist fanatics." Rosatstein advocated that boys should instead become socialists. The communists/socialists/Marxists continued their attacks on the Boy Scouts for years, with little success.

Kengor continues, "This runs all the way to modern times, especially as American communists vigorously embraced cultural issues. By the start of the new century—as seen, for instance, in a May 2001 issue of Party Builder—Communist Party USA was joining forces with the ACLU to openly condemn the Boy Scouts as 'anti-gay.'

"And alas, it was here that the far left found its formula. This tactic would work masterfully in redefining the Boy Scouts in the left's own image. As cultural Marxists have taught in their universities, the trick to deconstructing America, especially its Judeo-Christian roots, is to go cultural, not economic, particularly through the perverting of sexuality and gender. The key was a cultural Marxist revolution rather than an economic Marxist revolution. That's the ticket." [30]

The battle against the Boy Scout continued for years. To summarize the current situation, back in 2015, BSA president Robert Gates (yes, RINO Bush's man) led the BSA board to allow homosexual scout leaders.[31] This resulted in enough sexual abuse lawsuits to force the Boy Scouts of America to seek bankruptcy protection in 2000. The BSA has never been the same since.

It's tough to find an organization with a better legacy of not only promoting good deeds but also turning boys into men. Thanks to some evil forces, the Boy Scouts of America is now a confused shell of its former self.

---

[30] Paul Kengor, "The Left's War on Boy Scouts Has Raged for 100 Years," June 1, 2018, https://www.westernjournal.com/the-lefts-war-on-the-boy-scouts-has-raged-for-100-years/.

[31] "The Deep State Takedown of the Boy Scouts of America," February 19, 2018, https://www.scottlively.net/2020/02/19/the-deep-state-takedown-of-the-boy-scouts-of-america/.

CHAPTER 6

The Impact of the War on Masculinity on the Church

Since our churches are not doing a good job of practicing biblical separation from a corrosive culture, it is no surprise that the culture is heavily influencing the church instead of vice versa. Possibly, the most tragic and dangerous consequence of our culture's overall war on masculinity is that it is having an inordinate impact on church leadership.

Is Your Pastor a Coward?

One of the weaknesses of Christianity in the United States is this strange obsession with choosing our church pastors based on the number of college degrees they have. Some of the seminaries have been ideologically compromised, so it exacerbates the problem when churches hire pastors with multiple degrees. The other issue with seminaries, by their very nature, is that the people who are there are subsidized and insulated from real life. I believe that God has designed a lot of self-correction into our lives, but that self-correction gets short-circuited when somebody is not actually producing anything but is funded by donations or taxpayers. Seminaries are not exactly a recipe for promoting and increasing the masculinity of Christian men. I am convinced that one of the strengths of the historical Black church is that their pastors could not afford to be ruined by a seminary, so they were forced to simply study the Bible. The pastors also had to work a "real" job during the week, so they could relate to the "real" world.

A lot of pastors operate in a bubble that is only loosely connected to reality. These pastors like to work the same hours as the men in the church. So instead of waiting until the evening to communicate with the men in their church, they communicate with the most accessible members—the stay-at-home moms. At the end of the day, the pastors are ready to relax with their own families instead of working with the male church members. So if you made a pie chart of the amount of time during a week, Sunday to Saturday, that the average pastor talks to women versus talking with men, it would be heavily skewed toward the pastor spending most of his time communicating with women.

The net result is that not only do we have a doctrine problem, but we also have a courage problem.

Where Are the Tough Guys?

A lot of tough guys cannot attend your church because they are incarcerated. I am not saying to release all the prisoners or that the criminal justice system is a complete failure. But it is impossible to deny the impact of the incarceration rate of males on the decreasing level of masculinity in the church. I visited a megachurch recently. I decided to do a somewhat statistically significant count of the men and women in the section next to mine. The count was thirty-one women and nine men. It's tough to quantify how many men would go to church if they were not incarcerated. But if the incarceration rate is impacting the larger subset of the overall culture, it obviously impacts the number of men available to attend or be involved in church.

Let's look at some of the foundations of the incarceration problem:

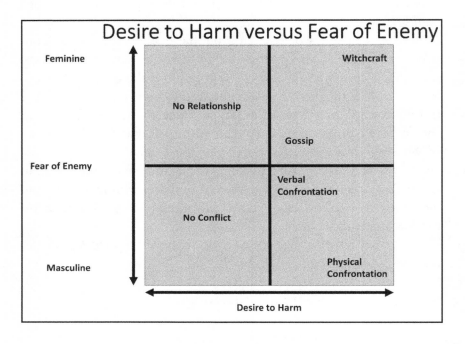

Fear of the enemy is more of a feminine trait, and that is why witchcraft has historically been associated with women. Witchcraft is always evil. Physical confrontations are often evil. Yet we incarcerate for physical confrontations and make movies that promote witchcraft. If we incarcerated people for the sin of gossip, the prison population would quickly become filled with old White women.

There is a model used in the auditing world to identify environments that are susceptible to financial fraud. The model is called the "fraud triangle,"[32] but it could also be called the "sin triangle." The model is based on a "three-legged stool" of conditions: incentive, opportunity, and rationalization. Basically, for financial fraud (or any other wrongdoing) to occur, there must be an incentive, the opportu-

---

[32] https://corporatefinanceinstitute.com/resources/knowledge/accounting/fraud-triangle/.

THE IDENTITY MATRIX

nity to commit the crime, and the ability to rationalize one's actions afterward. Applying the model to young males being incarcerated, thanks to NAFTA, many of the jobs for these young men have been offshored. Many of these young men are unchurched or have been under "hyper-grace" teaching, so it is easy for them to rationalize their actions. They are not going to be taught in public school about morality. The last leg of the stool is opportunity. With no father in the home, there are more opportunities for these young men to get into trouble.

Men are (still) expected to be the provider in their relationship(s). It is more profitable to sell illegal drugs than legal drugs due to the obvious legally restricted supply coupled with high demand. Also, the illegal nature of drug transactions makes them tax-free. That gives broke young men a double incentive to sell drugs. A lot of these young men end up incarcerated.

Another huge issue with incarceration that the mainstream media does not seem to care about is that American prisons are probably the most voluntarily racist places in the world. Most prisoners join a gang in prison that is based primarily on their racial identity. They will usually carry this gang affiliation with them when they leave prison. Prison is also a "criminal college" where young men are exposed to older hardened criminals who are experts at lawbreaking.

We should care deeply about the incarceration issue. A good resource is www.prisonfellowship.org.

The 501.c.3 Trap

United States Internal Revenue Code 501.c.3 is the section of IR code that regulates federal nonprofit organizations. These organizations are typically charities, private foundations, and churches. Because of 501.c.3 rules against lobbying and political activity, many churches are afraid to make statements or be involved with anything that seems even remotely political.

Here is an excerpt from a statement on the "Political Responsibility of Mitchell Road Presbyterian Church," Greenville, South Carolina:

> To teach each Christian that it is his responsibility to decide which proposed legislation, candidates for office, or political party best supports true religion, justice, and peace; to teach that all such decisions must be made with prayer, asking the Holy Spirit to enlighten their conscience by the Word of God; to teach that *such matters of conscience do not fall within the authority of the visible church; and to make it very clear that such matters of conscience are not in any way a condition of fellowship with other believers at Mitchell Road Presbyterian Church.* To remind those who serve in public office that civil government has its authority from God and, therefore, those who hold public office will surely answer to God for their exercise of that authority; to remind the civil government that it must do what God commands, that it must not do what God forbids, but that it may do whatever else is not forbidden; and should the civil government fail in its duties to God, to publicly make that indiscretion known on the basis of God's Word. And finally, in committing ourselves to a practical application of these truths we, the members of Mitchell Road Presbyterian Church, will also refrain from: Using our stated worship services for patriotic rallies, honor guard ceremonies, political action statements, or as a forum for the support of political candidates; conducting voter registration, providing forms for voter registration, or distributing voter guides; and *from all other political*

*activities which are the duties and privileges of indi-
vidual citizens but are not functions of the church.*

This statement is most likely motivated by a desire to protect
the church's 501.c.3 tax-exempt status. But it is obvious that statements like this will weaken any moral message the church might have
regarding speaking to a moral issue that is also a political issue, such
as abortion.

The Feminized Church

It stands to reason that feminized people would seek out feminized churches. Rollo Tomassi says in his book *The Rational Male:
Religion*, "Since the mid 80's, the most sustainable profit model in
mainstream religions follow a similar template:

- Be sensitive to the secular needs of women
- Foster a church culture of female empowerment
- Find contemporary ways to be relevant to women outside
  the belief structure
- Reward and reinforce the appreciation of women's experi-
  ence and struggle
- Appeal to and affirm the emotional nature of women
- Remove judgmentalism and reassign responsibility for
  women's sins to irresponsible men
- Make covert feminist ideology kosher and later an identify-
  ing characteristic of that religious franchise

"This template for church success has become so endemic that
even the most recognizable personalities in mainstream church cultures don't realize they play a party to it. The formula has always
been the lens which they consider faith, so even questioning it seems
wrong."

In his article "A Feminized Faith," P. Andrew Sandlin says,
"Feminism is essentially a false religion warring against historical

Christianity. By a feminized faith, however, I refer not merely to the organized goddess religion of allegedly Protestant churches: this expression of feminist religion is obvious. I refer mainly to the feminized religion practiced by sissy evangelicals, curling-iron conservatives, and the blandly (but not truly) Reformed, among many others. These suffer from syncretism; they attempt to reconcile Biblical Christianity with an alien faith. There are several indelible marks of this feminized faith." Here are the characteristics that Sandlin describes:

1) Relational rather than theological: "A feminized faith substitutes man's relationship with a man not merely for man's relationship to God but also for the very objectivity of the faith. What becomes important in the church, therefore, is not its fidelity to the teachings of Scripture (which, to be sure, includes the proper relationship between our brethren), but the camaraderie among the members."

2) Domestic rather than dominant: "Second, feminized faith stresses the domestic rather than the dominant. The woman's principal calling is her home—and any other calling must be subordinate to that calling (Titus 2:5). But man's calling is primarily external to the home—active dominion (and, of course, woman assists the man in his dominion task by exerting dominion in the domestic realm). Because of this calling, man is inherently conquest-oriented while woman is inherently nurture-oriented. This is an aspect of the creation order that all of the finely spun theories of frenzied feminism cannot obliterate. It is imperative to recognize that the religion of feminism works not merely to transform woman to the image of man but to transform man into the image of woman. Feminism is, therefore, a religious perversion. Its goal is not "equality" with men but the transformation of biblical manhood and womanhood. It strikes at the heart of God's creation order. It seeks, therefore, to masculinize women and feminize (or at least emas-

culate) men. A feminized faith is, therefore, a domesticated faith. It is not interested in a world-conquering vision in the name of King Jesus but in a severe navel contemplation within the four walls of the institutional church. If evangelical, it frames "seeker-sensitive" churches, glib and emotional "praise" music, and tepid, baby sitting pastors. If it is Reformed, Lutheran, or Presbyterian, it obsesses itself with the procedures of the church, synods, and general assemblies and neglects the virile dominionist task of taking back from Satan the territory he has expropriated from Christ and his church."

3) Subordination rather than leadership: "The feminized faith renders the church subordinate to society rather than a leader of society. Within the church, there is no firm, decisive leadership since the pastor (of either sex) works for servitude, camaraderie, and consensus rather than bold, daring, advancing objectives. This generally reduces to the proposition of making the congregation happy at all costs. The feminized faith in its broader implications stifles any impetus to cultural leadership. The Christians and church are no longer a city set on a hill, a beacon of righteousness in the community, but rather a little po' folk toddle-along nursery conforming to the cultural mores and slapping on a Christian label for good measure."[33]

Let's look at the Christian church (personified) on the Personal Identity Matrix. Churches tend to be in the box that I have drawn on the matrix. To put some boundaries on the "church box," let's start with a quote from a very unlikely source—DL Hughley, "Black church is the gayest place on the face of the earth...it's women, children, and gay dudes. Women going to pray for a man, children who gotta go with their women..." and I'll stop there to keep it clean. That means there is a range of masculine and feminine churches.

---

[33] P. Andrew Sandlin. "A Feminized Faith," February 1, 1998. https://chalcedon.edu/magazine/a-feminized-faith.

Feminine churches may or may not be led by a female. But feminine churches are quite common and have some distinctive traits that appear harmless. One characteristic is that they love to decorate everything. They like to decorate and redecorate for every event. Some of this is not bad to remind us of Christmas or Easter, but you can tell that much of the conversations in the church staff meeting that we started off with revolve around decorating. I have read various estimates that women tend to spend over the course of their lifetime tens of thousands and as high as $250,000 on makeup, hair care, and cosmetic products. If you're in a feminine church, you will see a whole lot of cosmetics going on. Feminine churches also love social events. There is also an emphasis on rallying around causes that are deemed good and non-offensive. That's where you see things like the Blessing of the Animals. Feminine churches have a tough time saying no to almost any perceived cause, victim, or underdog. A trait of toxic femininity is an obsession with externalities. This is why a lot of pastors of very feminized churches dress like pimps.

There are a lot of solid, godly pastors out there who have given up so much to do their job, and they're doing a great job. But a lot of pastors are not. If your pastor is a coward, we need to analyze why that is. The litmus test for a lot of these feminized pastors is a complete absence of conflict in every single ministry or relationship of that church. You will hear Christians say that we cannot ever have an "us versus them" mentality. That statement occurs nowhere in the Bible. Peacemaking is misunderstood, and compromising has taken its place. The problem with compromising is that if you are attempting to compromise with an evil person, all they need to do is continue to over time become more and more evil, and they will pull you in their direction. The obsession with avoiding all conflict plays out in the absence of church discipline. The lack of church discipline can result in many wolves in sheep's clothing being a part of a local congregation and working against what that church is supposed to be working for. Another thing to look at is whether the whole Bible is being preached. If the "Holy Grail," as it were for these feminine churches, is the avoidance of conflict, a lot of Bible verses will never be seen or heard in that church. In a feminine organization, policy is often determined by whoever throws the biggest temper tantrum. A lot of these feminine local churches have women's conferences that tend to have the same theme—it's always all about empowering or transforming women. Most of these conferences are attempting to move women down and to the right on the matrix. They are trying to influence women to be more masculine. A feminized church will rarely do any mission work. It will be called mission work, but it will be more standard charity work than evangelism.

Any feminized organization will respond to external threats and stimuli in a similar manner. There is an underlying philosophy of "if you are nice to them, they'll be nice to you." That means that the typical response to any potential conflict is to be "nicer." The number one goal is to avoid conflict at all costs. This also means that there will be almost no church discipline because it seems messy and judgmental. It also takes courage to administer church discipline. Feminine organizations will also try to put down anyone who iden-tifies a potential threat as overreacting or that the person identifying the threat is a troublemaker.

The net result of the war on masculinity in the Christian church is that the church is now almost completely unable to defend itself against external threats. The other result is that most churches are more motivated by becoming underdog advocates than by figuring out who is right and who is wrong. The way to manipulate these churches is to present your cause as being the underdog cause so you can more easily obtain their support. Many churches are now far more concerned with being (perceived) victim advocacy centers and "Social Justice centers" than in fulfilling the great commission.

The new rules of the feminine church:

1) Thou shalt not fight back or have any disagreements or conflicts.
2) Any legitimate evil or external threat will be discounted, minimized, or denied. Anyone who resists will be labeled an extremist.

WILLIAM WELLINGTON

3) Thou shalt not advocate truth.

4) Thou shalt not talk about law, politics, or religion (yes, religion).

5) Should any conflict occur, thou shalt side against the straight, masculine male, or if there is not one involved, thou shalt side strongly with the perceived underdog.

6) Thou shalt support and applaud poor performance and bad behavior.

7) The standard of right and wrong is determined either by the path of least resistance or by a hierarchy of perceived victimhood.

8) It is more important to tell people what they want to hear than to speak the truth.

9) If anything in the Bible seems "not very nice," then that is not to be mentioned.

10) It is more important to decorate over the chaos than to bring order to the chaos.

Once a church has been feminized, the door is now open for the next phase of the attack—Trojan horses.

CHAPTER 7

Trojan Horses

Did you notice that Social Justice warriors and Critical Race theorists showed up in churches at almost the same time that Antifa and Black Lives Matter started rioting in the streets? One of the things I hope to accomplish with this book is to give you some real analytical tools (unlike Critical Race Theory) that enable you to see the endgame of some of the cultural forces around you without having to spend too much time "connecting the dots" on who is doing the influencing. I do encourage you to do some research on the connections between the current religious "thought leaders" and the New World Order. A simple internet search on "Tim Keller Soros" will give you plenty to research. But suffice it to say, the way that Social Justice and Critical Race Theory have suddenly become fad theology simultaneously at the major seminaries, large denominations, and megachurches is no coincidence. These movements take money, and the money trail leads to some suspicious characters.

Keep in mind that some people trying to influence the church think they are being "peacemakers" and doing good. Also, keep in mind that most of them think that the end always justifies the means. But their means are abominable. Here is what Proverbs 6:16–19 says, "There are six things which the Lord hates, Yes, seven which are an abomination to Him: haughty eyes, a lying tongue, and hands that shed innocent blood, a heart that devises wicked plans, feet that run rapidly to evil, a false witness who utters lies, and one who spreads strife among brothers."

In the New Testament, the church is commanded to be salt and light. In order to build the New World Order, the church must be weakened. A key component of that goal is the Trojan horse strategy.

The Story of the Trojan Horse

While the story of the Trojan horse is fictional, it describes a brilliant military strategy that is still used today. Computers are attacked daily by "trojan horse" malware, for example. A good summary of the mythical Trojan horse story comes from *Encyclopedia Britannica*:

> [The] Trojan horse, [was a] huge hollow wooden horse constructed by the Greeks to gain entrance into Troy during the Trojan War. The horse was built by Epeius, a master carpenter and pugilist. The Greeks, pretending to desert the war, sailed to the nearby island of Tenedos, leaving behind Sinon, who persuaded the Trojans that the horse was an offering to Athena (goddess of war) that would make Troy impregnable. Despite the warnings of Laocoön and Cassandra, the horse was taken inside the city gates. That night, Greek warriors emerged from it and opened the gates to let in the returned Greek army. The story is told at length in Book II of the Aeneid and is touched upon in the Odyssey. The term Trojan horse has come to refer to subversion introduced from the outside. Beginning in the late 20th century, the name "Trojan horse" was applied to deceptively benign computer codes that seem like legitimate applications but are written to damage or disrupt a computer's programming or to steal personal information.

I highly recommend the 2004 movie *Troy*, directed by Wolfgang Petersen, for a vivid depiction of the effectiveness of the Trojan horse strategy.

Lessons from the Trojan horse story:

1) It was new.
2) It was free.
3) It promised peace.
4) It distracted the target from the real threat.
5) It minimized the real threat.
6) It showed up with nobody asking for it.
7) It looked good on the outside.
8) It did not work alone. It worked for the hostile force.
9) The men inside the Trojan horse were valued for stealth.
10) The primary mission of the Trojan horse was to open the gate to a hostile force.
11) It was coordinated to be a kill shot.
12) Eventually, the target was defeated.

As we look at how various Trojan horses have been used against the church, you will see how many of these same dynamics are in play today.

The Virus Strategy

The COVID-19 virus changed the world starting in 2019. This pandemic prompted virtually every adult in the world to want to learn more about viruses. The first thing you learn about a virus is that it is not a living cell. There is an entire scientific debate about whether a virus is a life-form. We do know that a virus is an infinitesimally small package of devastatingly bad information. That bad information is then used to modify healthy cells in such a way that they are not only destroyed, but in the process, they manufacture more viruses.

From the movie *Inception*, "an idea is like a virus, resilient, highly contagious. The smallest seed of an idea can grow. It can grow to define or destroy you."

The virus strategy was prophesied in the Bible with the "wolves in sheep's clothing" and "false prophets" passages. A wolf wants to change your beliefs, behavior, destroy you, or all the above. Here are the New Testament passages that address wolves in sheep's clothing:

> Beware of the false prophets, who come to you in sheep's clothing, but inwardly are ravenous wolves. (Matthew 7:15)

> I know that after my departure savage wolves will come in among you, not sparing the flock; and from among your own selves men will arise, speaking perverse things, to draw away the disciples after them. (Acts 20:29–30)

> Many false prophets will arise and will mislead many. Because lawlessness is increased, most people's love will grow cold. (Matthew 24:11–12)

> Notice the connection between love and law. A war on law is a war on love.

> For false Christs and false prophets will arise and will show great signs and wonders, so as to mislead, if possible, even the elect. (Matthew 24:24)

> But false prophets also arose among the people, just as there will also be false teachers among you, who will secretly introduce destructive heresies, even denying the Master who bought them, bringing swift destruction upon themselves. Many will follow their sensuality, and because of them the

way of the truth will be maligned and in their greed they will exploit you with false words; their judgment from long ago is not idle, and their destruction is not asleep. For if God did not spare angels when they sinned, but cast them into hell and committed them to pits of darkness, reserved for judgment; and did not spare the ancient world, but preserved Noah, a preacher of righteousness, with seven others, when He brought a flood upon the world of the ungodly; and if He condemned the cities of Sodom and Gomorrah to destruction by reducing them to ashes, having made them an example to those who would live ungodly lives thereafter; and if He rescued righteous Lot, oppressed by the sensual conduct of unprincipled men (for by what he saw and heard that righteous man, while living among them, felt his righteous soul tormented day after day by their lawless deeds), then the Lord knows how to rescue the godly from temptation, and to keep the unrighteous under punishment for the day of judgment, and especially those who indulge the flesh in its corrupt desires and despise authority. Daring, self-willed, they do not tremble when they revile angelic majesties, whereas angels who are greater in might and power do not bring a reviling judgment against them before the Lord. But these, like unreasoning animals, born as creatures of instinct to be captured and killed, reviling where they have no knowledge, will in the destruction of those creatures also be destroyed, suffering wrong as the wages of doing wrong. They count it a pleasure to revel in the daytime. They are stains and blemishes, reveling in their deceptions, as they carouse with you, having eyes full of adultery that never cease from sin, enticing unstable souls, having a heart trained in greed, accursed children; forsaking the right way, they have gone astray, having followed the way of Balaam, the son of Beor, who loved the wages of unrighteousness; but he received a rebuke for his own transgression, for a mute donkey, speaking with a voice of a man, restrained the madness of the prophet. These are springs without water and mists driven by a storm, for whom the black darkness has been reserved. For speaking out arrogant words of vanity they entice by fleshly desires, by sensuality, those who barely escape from the ones who live in error, promising them freedom while they themselves are slaves of corruption; for by what a man is overcome, by this he is enslaved. For if, after they have escaped the defilements of the world by the knowledge of the Lord and Savior Jesus Christ, they are again entangled in them and are overcome, the last state has become worse for them than the first. For it would be better for them not to have known the way of righteousness, than having known it, to turn away from the holy commandment handed on to them. It has happened to them according to the true proverb, "A dog returns to its own vomit," and "A sow, after washing, returns to wallowing in the mire." (2 Peter 2:1–22)

Types of infiltrators (wolves in sheep's clothing)—some are clergy, some are not:

1) The science guy: this person passes himself off as knowing far more about science than your pastor (or the Bible). The objective of "the science guy" is to look at the first chapter

of the Bible and say, "Did God really say that?" The science guy is trying to attack the belief in the inerrancy of scripture.

2) The Social Justice warrior
3) The happy musician: the happy musician is put on stage due to a high level of music skill but will typically wear feminine clothes if male and masculine clothes if female.
4) The metrosexual
5) The "everything is awesome!" prosperity pastor
6) The black hole: this person is some sort of victim who will use inordinate church resources. These are usually attractive females.
7) The systematic theology expert: this person is usually a pastor who spends more time talking about systematic theology than the Bible.

The chart below shows various cultural forces that are attacking the Christian church from the outside, and the corresponding Trojan horse that is trying to work from inside the church.

Cultural Force	Trojan Horse
Feminism	"Christian Feminism"
LGBT	"SSA Christian" movement
Antifa	Social Justice Movement
Black Lives Matter	Critical Race Theory
Witchcraft	Yoga
Marxism	Liberation Theology

Table 10 Cultural forces and Trojan horses

Masculine Christian men are uniquely qualified to identify, call out, resist, and excommunicate wolves in sheep's clothing and false prophets.

The New "Morality"

Morality used to be all about discovering truth and applying it to life. Modern culture has a few foundational principles that are being exported to the church:

1) Always blindly support the underdog because "underdogs" are inherently righteous.
2) It is good to tell "helpful" lies and censor "harmful" truth.
3) Telling someone anything they don't want to hear is "hate speech," even if it is a Bible verse.

Foundational to the new "morality" is a war on truth, which is essentially repetitive deception. It's probably safest for me to quote from the Bible at this point. This is from Matthew chapter 24, verses 4 through 13.

> And Jesus answered and said unto them, Take heed that no man deceive you. For many shall come in my name, saying, I am Christ; and shall deceive many. And ye shall hear of wars and rumors of wars: see that ye be not troubled: for all these things must come to pass, but the end is not yet. For nation shall rise against nation, and kingdom against kingdom: and there shall be famines, and pestilences, and earthquakes, in diverse places. All these are the beginning of sorrows. Then shall they deliver you up to be afflicted, and shall kill you: and ye shall be hated of all nations for my name's sake. And then shall many be offended, and shall betray one another and shall hate one another. And many false prophets shall rise, and shall deceive many. And because iniquity shall abound, the love of many

shall wax cold. But he that shall endure unto the
end, the same shall be saved.

You can see in the previous passage that Jesus begins with both a
warning and a commandment to not be deceived. So what is deception? Deception is either getting someone to believe something that
is not true or to get them to believe that something that is true is
not really true. The first deception on record is recorded in Genesis
chapter 3, verses 1 through 6.

> Now the serpent was more subtle than any beast
> of the field which the Lord God had made. And
> he said unto the woman, yea, hath God said, you
> shall not eat of every tree of the garden? And the
> woman said unto the serpent, we may eat of the
> fruit of the trees of the garden: but of the fruit
> of the tree which is in the midst of the garden,
> God has said, ye shall not eat of it, neither shall
> ye touch it, lest you die. And the serpent said
> unto the woman, ye shall not surely die: for God
> doth know that in the day ye eat thereof, then
> your eyes shall be opened, and ye shall be as gods,
> knowing good and evil. And when the woman
> saw that the tree was good for food, and that it
> was pleasant to the eyes, and a tree to be desired
> to make one wise, she took of the fruit thereof,
> and did eat, and gave also unto her husband with
> her; and he did eat.

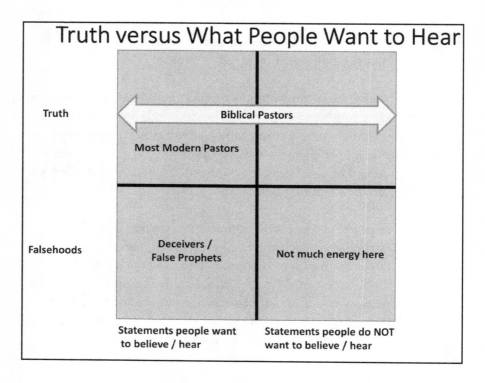

The matrix above has two axes—truth versus falsehoods and things people want to hear/believe versus things people do not want to hear or believe. There is not a lot of energy around things that are false that people do not want to believe. This is the lower right quadrant. The upper right quadrant—the truth that people want to believe (and hear) is the wheelhouse for most modern megachurch pastors. Joel Osteen, TD Jakes, Kenneth Copeland, Steven Furtick all operate almost exclusively in this quadrant. The lower left quadrant—falsehoods that people want to believe (and hear) is where impostor pastors, liberal pastors, deceivers, and false prophets operate. The current pope seems to be working in this quadrant as of late. There are very few pastors today who will speak truths that people do not want to believe (or hear). But that is exactly what prepares people for the gospel.

"Science" versus the Bible

In an effort to attack the inerrancy of Scripture, the Bible is often attacked by "science." When you drill down on these attacks, you can see that the "science" is either fraudulent or selectively used.

	Abortion	Sexual Identity	Creation
Bible says:	Life begins at conception.	God created people male and female.	God created the earth in six days.
Science says:	An unborn baby is alive.	Sex is determined by chromosomes.	No transitional form has ever been found. Evolution remains a theory.
Modern culture says:	Reproductive rights are a choice.	Sex is determined by individual choice.	Evolution is a scientific fact.
Your pastor says:	Probably nothing.	Probably nothing.	Probably pleads ignorance.

Table 11. Attacking the Bible with "science."

Legitimate science proves that abortion is murder and that sex/gender is determined by a Y chromosome. Legitimate science admits that the process of a caterpillar turning into a butterfly is enough of an issue for the theory of evolution to collapse the whole theory. So do not be intimidated by fake "science."

The "Christian Feminists"

There are groups such as CBE (Christians for Biblical Equality) who ostensibly are working to correct thousands of years of "inequality" and "discrimination" against women in the church. Allegedly, all these injustices are caused by past incorrect interpretations of the Bible. The "Christian feminists" are not motivated by The Great Commission. They are primarily motivated by putting women in power positions in the church. They do a lot of logical gymnastics to try to make the Bible say what they want it to say. It seems like every women's conference for the past five years has been called "Empowering Women."

"Love" as the Apex Virtue

Before we move into the next section, it's important to define love. Is it more important to tell someone what they want to hear or what they need to hear? The correct answer should be based on what is at stake. If someone asks you if their outfit makes them look fat, the correct answer is probably "no," because, in reality, it is their fat that makes them look fat, not their outfit. We are all aware that our bodies could use some improvement in some way, so it's not a big deal. However, historically, people have become so angry as to commit murder if someone tells them they are on a path to hell. Everyone who is on a path to hell needs to be told, but most do not want to be told. Love is having the courage to lovingly tell them they are on a path to hell. In 2021, this message most often applies to how Christians relate to LGBTQ people. I love LGBTQ people. Most Christians really do, believe it or not. However, the LGBTQ as a collective is determined to silence any message that they (LGBTQ) are on a dangerous eternal path. They want the authority to criminalize the people who are trying to save them.

"Love" has been redefined by universally accepting everyone, regardless of their behavior. "Love" has also been redefined by only telling people what they want to hear. This contradicts Scripture.

> And this is love, that we walk according to His commandments. This is the commandment, just as you have heard from the beginning, that you should walk in it. (2 John 1:6)

LGBTQ and the "SSA Christian" Movement

God is a separator, a sanctifier, and a divider. Satan likes to unite things that don't belong together. Satan would like to completely unite the LGBTQ community and the church, including your church. But in order to do that, your church has to change. This time, a "baby steps" approach will be used. It will be a gateway issue, much like "rape and incest" were used to start moving the needle on the abortion debate. "Same-sex attraction" (SSA) has been chosen to be the gateway issue for getting the church to embrace the LGBTQ community. But again, since there are sticky wickets in the church like the story of Sodom and Gomorrah, your church will have to change first.

Here are the core tenets of the SSA Christian movement:

1) SSA does not stem from early trauma and is always unchosen, very possibly inborn.
2) Conversion to Christianity does not necessarily remove this attraction, which may be lifelong.
3) Same-sex attractions are not sinful if not fleshed out.
4) The church is historically guilty of deeply oppressing and alienating this group.
5) All sins are equal, and same-sex sexual attraction is a sin like any other. [34]

Let's look at this in reverse order. We will cover the fifth point in the next section titled "Sin Like No Other." The fourth point is cultural Marxism. The third point is a lie that contradicts what Jesus said about heterosexual attraction. The second point contradicts the Biblical command for sanctification. The first point leads with two lies and ends with a truth (very possibly inborn) that would align with the doctrine of original sin.

Since you now know that this movement is yet another attempt to move you to the wrong place on the Personal Identity Matrix, the only correct response is to not give an inch. The SSA crowd has the freedom to start their own church. They don't need you to change yours.

---

[34] Rebecca McLaughlin, "Gospelizing Idolatry at TGC Part II," 2018, https://enemieswithinthechurch.com/.

Sin Like No Other

When a pastor does preach about homosexuality and/or transgender behavior, they are often quick to say that "we are all sinners" and act like these sins are no worse than any other sins. Let's look at that assumption:

Sin	Form the person's identity	Externally signal the person's identity	Band together as a collective	Lobby for preferred civil rights status	Lobby to limit religious liberty	Try to force everyone to say their behavior is good	Try to punish anyone who does not believe like they do
Murder							
Adultery		•					
Fornication							
Lying							
Substance Abuse	•		•				
Stealing							
Homosexuality	•		•	•	•	•	•
Transgender	•	•	•	•	•	•	•

Table 12. Comparing sins.

It is probably wishful thinking that leads a lot of pastors to preach that homosexuality and transgender are no bigger deal than lying or stealing. The pastors that do have the courage to speak about these topics are once again trying to compromise to try to get everyone to just get along. The LGBTQ group does not want these sins to be treated like any other sin, so why do preachers act like these sins are just like any other sins? The ultimate goal of the far right column in the chart above is to criminalize Christianity.

I once knew a man who had come out of homosexuality. He said that there was a time in his life when he was deep in the LGBTQ movement and that he wanted to contract HIV or AIDS because he thought it would help him get to the inner circle of that movement. Have you ever heard of an alcoholic who wanted to contract cirrhosis of the liver because they thought it would get him to the inner circle of alcoholics?

LGBTQ wants to know if you are an ally or not. That sounds awfully binary. What if you are a trans-ally? What if your "Q" in LGBTQ stands for "Questioning?" Are you allowed to question LGBTQ?

Most churches have completely whiffed on biblical sexual identity. "Whom are you attracted to?" is trumping biblical identity. Let's look at some verses.

> The woman shall not wear that which pertaineth unto a man, neither shall a man put on a woman's garment: for all that do so are abomination unto the Lord thy God. (Deuteronomy 22:5)

> Thou shalt not lie with mankind, as with womankind: it is an abomination. (Leviticus 18:22)

> Know ye not that the unrighteous shall not inherit the kingdom of God? Be not deceived, neither fornicators, nor idolaters, nor adulterers, nor effeminate, nor abusers of themselves with mankind, nor thieves nor covetous, nor drunkards, nor revilers, nor extortioners, shall inherit the kingdom of God. (I Corinthians 6:9–10)

First of all, yes, most of those are Old Testament verses. But there is absolutely no evidence that Jesus came to overturn them. There is no evidence of anything described as an abomination in the Old Testament that Jesus came and said it's now okay. An abomination then is an abomination now. The LGBTQ people call the verses above "clobber verses." However, if a truth can be used to prevent you from going to hell, it's not a "clobber verse." It's a love verse. A lot of churches copped out early on the LGBTQ issue by focusing on the concept that people cannot help whom they are attracted to.

Let's look at a chart of sexual identity and sexual orientation for men:

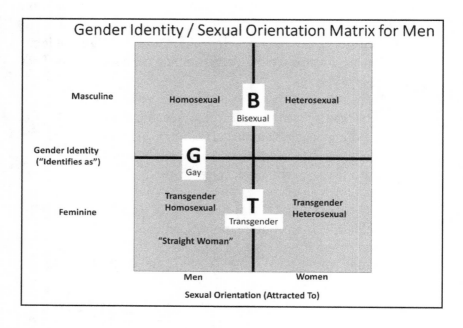

To show you how messy things can get when you deviate from God's design, let's look at a man who (tries to) identify as a woman but who is still attracted to women. Bruce Jenner is the most well-known example. Who can forget his interview with Diane Sawyer when Sawyer asked Jenner, "Are you a lesbian?"

By focusing on the upper left quadrant (men who identify as men but are attracted to men) and then conceding it, a lot of churches and denominations ended up conceding the lower two quadrants as well.

Now churches are giving tacit approval to these abominations by refusing to talk about them. A lot of churches have gotten to the point where they now actively promote the homosexual agenda.

A real danger of contradicting biblical directions for church purity and bringing the LGBTQ-etc. people into your church is that they identify as LGBTQ-etc. first and as Christians, second. Instead of starting their own church, they would rather change or destroy yours. Don't be surprised if churches who cave on biblical sexuality start paying for gender reassignment surgery. Of course, these payments will be called "love," so that if you don't "affirm" it, you will be accused of being "hateful."

The idea of separation of church and state has also played out in such a way that Christians have opted out of being involved in politics. It's interesting that the same people who told us for a long time that you can't legislate morality are now heavily invested in trying to legislate immorality. We will look at this issue deeper in a few chapters to see how the LGBTQ is already trying to weaponize civil government against the church.

The Gospel Coalition

Organizations are started to try to accomplish something big. Sometimes, secret societies will claim that their reason for existence is partying, but you can party with your neighbors. Sometimes, the goal of an organization is to change other organizations. Somebody had to build the ideological Trojan horses and convince the churches to pull them inside. A major force in doing that has been The Gospel Coalition, the Wuhan Lab of American Christianity.

The Gospel Coalition was founded in 2005 by D. A. Carson and Tim Keller. It has succeeded in creating an online echo chamber where the Gospel Coalition pastors constantly retweet, share, like, and otherwise cheer on and promote each other's radical ideas. It has now reached the point that other pastors judge their success or failure by the approval of this online ideological oligarchy instead of seeking and obeying God's will.

In a recent bombshell report, Pulpit & Pen demonstrated "how Democratic financier and organizer Zack Exley is behind the successful attempt to change the political ideology of America's major evangelical institutions, ministries, and seminaries through the propagation of what is known as 'Social Justice.'"

Here is a summary of the report: [35]

---

[35] "BOMBSHELL: 'Justice Democrats' Founder Is the Organizer of Evangelical Social Justice Movement," July 29, 2019, https://pulpitandpen.org/2019/07/29/

We will explain—with a compilation of original sources, some of which have been recovered
after they were deleted from the Internet—the
driving political force behind the takeover of
America's Reformed evangelical community and
demonstrate the money ties between a powerful Democratic financier and evangelical leaders
who are steering churches into progressive ideology for political purposes.

Far from being an organic, Bible-driven
movement, the ideas presented at institutions
like Southeastern Baptist Theological Seminary,
Southern Baptist Theological Seminary, Midwestern
Baptist Theological Seminary, 9 Marks, Together
for the Gospel, the Ethics and Religious Liberty
Commission, and The Gospel Coalition are driven
by a gameplan orchestrated by Exley, and the purpose is to keep evangelicals from voting Republican
in the upcoming 2020 election cycle.

There is no doubt that Reformed evangelicalism—historically, a bastion of conservative
Christianity—has been overtaken by "woke" Social
Justice ideology over the course of the last several years. Many people have wondered why so
many formerly conservative leaders and entities—
especially those related to the Southern Baptist
Convention and the parachurch ministry, The
Gospel Coalition—have converted almost entirely
to an ideology that seems sympatico with the talking
points of the Democratic Party. Research conducted
by Pulpit & Pen now has the answer as to how this
coordinated effort to turn Reformed evangelicalism
to the political left has been accomplished.

bombshell-justice-democrats-founder-is-the-organizer-of-evangelical-social-
justice-movement/.

The Gospel Coalition has taken advantage of the modern obsession with "star power" to attempt to centralize the ideology of Protestant Christianity in America by forming a club of ecclesiastical elites. Christianity now has its own internal woke mob. It's called the Gospel Coalition.

Aborting Trump

The 2020 presidential election was a litmus test of the thoughts and motives of many of our "leading" pastors and theologians.

Here is a chart of the major issues in the election, along with the positions of the two candidates, Joe Biden and Donald Trump.

Issue	Biden	Trump
Abortion	For unrestricted abortion, even late-term.	Has limited taxpayer funding to Planned Parenthood, generally against abortion.
COVID	Position is basically the same as Trumps, except that Biden openly advocates more mask mandates and lockdowns, especially for churches, but not for riots.	Poured record federal assistance into fighting the COVID pandemic.
Religious Freedom	Kamala Harris openly advocates "marriage equality". If elected this will probably mean shutting down churches who do not perform same-sex weddings.	Has supported the rights of churches to defend a one man/one woman position on marriage.
Economy	Generally advocates socialism at every opportunity.	Defends free markets from unfair competition from China. Minority unemployment was at record low before COVID.
Immigration	Open borders.	Defends borders, advocates merit-based immigration.
Civil Unrest	Has yet to denounce Antifa / BLM riots	Has offered federal support to end riots.
Healthcare	Generally advocates socialism at every opportunity.	Supports free market healthcare.
Law Enforcement	Expected to reduce funding and legal support of local police.	Supports local law enforcement.
Second Amendment	Against gun rights.	Pro gun rights.
Social Justice	Guarantee transgender students access to facilities based on their gender identity instead of scientific facts like their sex.	Passed the most comprehensive criminal justice reform in decades. 91% of those released from prison due to this legislation have been black.
Voter Accountability	Policies promote election anarchy.	Supports accountability in voting.
Military	Cut defense spending. Also ban veterans from using benefits at non-public education institutions (private or Christian colleges).	Has proven to support a strong military.

Table 14. Trump and Biden on the issues.

There are two ways to judge a political candidate, politically and personally.

Here is a comparison of Biden and Trump on the Personal Identity Matrix:

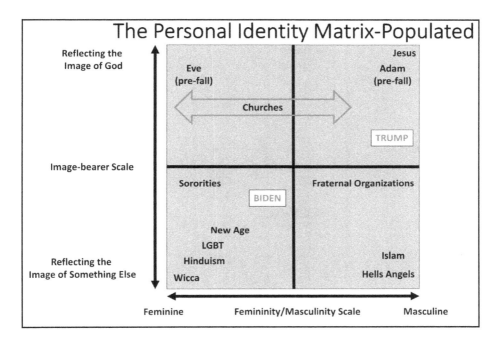

Here is a comparison of Biden and Trump on the Political Identity Matrix:

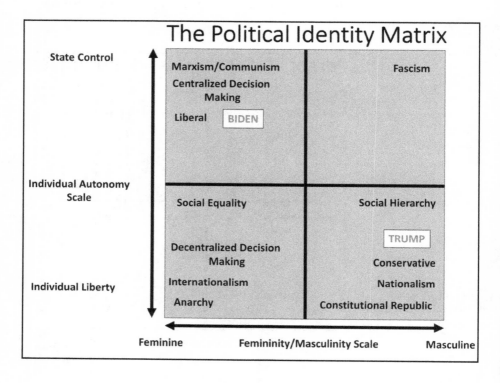

Not only was the 2020 presidential election a golden opportunity for the church, but it could also very well be critical to the survival of the church in the United States. One would expect almost universal and enthusiastic support for Donald Trump from Christians.

But instead, the most influential pastors broadcast almost the same message at the same time. The message was veiled but strong. The message was "It's okay to not vote for Trump, and it's okay to vote for Biden." Here are some examples:

Mark Dever ominously tweeted on August 18, 2020, "While we should work to end both voter fraud and voter suppression, neither voter fraud nor voter suppression in this coming November's elections will delegitimize the results."

Ed Stetzer tweeted on September 30, 2020, "It is stunning, but sadly not surprising, that the reflexive response of this president is, when asked to condemn white supremacy, to change the subject."

Jemar Tisby went even further and implied that it is evil to support Trump. He tweeted on October 10, 2020, "Any further work I do about Christian complicity and compromise with injustice will have to include Mike Pence as a paradigmatic example. We get a Tr*mp [sic] because of the cooperation and co-signing of people like Pence."

JD Greear tweeted on September 30, 2020, "When asked to condemn white supremacy, every single one of us should be ready to do so. Racism is, sadly, not extinct, and we know from our Southern Baptist history the effects of the horrific sins of racism and hatred."

Tim Keller tweeted on October 30, 2020, "Nevertheless, while believers can register under a party affiliation and be active in politics, they should not identify the Christian church or faith with a political party as the only Christian one…"

John Piper seems to have a slightly more active conscience than the other so-called Christian leaders, so he really had to talk himself into this one. Piper posted this on his Desiring God website on October 22, 2020. It reads in some sections like a suicide note and in other sections like it was written by someone being held hostage by terrorists:

> This article is probably as close as you will get to an answer on how I will vote in the upcoming presidential election.
>
> Probably?
>
> Right. Only God knows what may happen in the next days.
>
> Nothing I say here is intended to dictate how anyone else should vote but rather to point to a perspective that seems to be neglected. Yes,

this perspective sways my vote. [John, you later tweeted that you are not voting, what's up?] But you need not be sinning if you weigh matters differently.

Actually, this is a long-overdue article attempting to explain why I remain baffled that so many Christians consider the sins of unrepentant sexual immorality (porneia), unrepentant boastfulness (alazoneia), unrepentant vulgarity (aischrologia), unrepentant factiousness (dichostasiai), and the like, to be only toxic for our nation, while policies that endorse baby-killing, sex-switching, freedom-limiting, and socialistic overreach are viewed as deadly.

The reason I put those Greek words in parentheses is to give a graphic reminder that these are sins mentioned in the New Testament. To be more specific, they are sins that destroy people. They are not just deadly. They are deadly forever. They lead to eternal destruction (II Thessalonians 1:9).

They destroy persons (Acts 12:20–23). And through persons, they destroy nations (Jeremiah 48:29–31, 42).

Forgiveness through Christ is always possible where there is repentance and childlike trust in Jesus. But where humble repentance is absent, the sins condemn.

The New Testament teaches that "those who do such things will not inherit the kingdom of

God" (Galatians 5:21) and that "those who practice such things deserve to die" (Romans 1:32).

To which you may say, "So what? Rejecting
Jesus as Lord also leads to death, but you are willing to vote for a non-Christian, aren't you?" I am,
assuming there is enough overlap between biblical uprightness and the visible outworking of his
character and convictions. [John, you are really
dancing here. You have never been concerned
about the Clintons, Obama, or the behavior of
any other public figure. Why are you singling out
Trump?]

My point so far is simply to raise the stakes
of what is outwardly modeled in leadership, so
that Christians are given pause. It is not a small
thing to treat lightly a pattern of public behaviors
that lead to death.

In fact, I think it is a drastic mistake to think
that the deadly influences of a leader come only
through his policies and not also through his person. [Author's note: John, you are clearly making a moral judgment that Biden has the moral
high ground over Trump. Is this because he lies,
cheats, and steals, but he is "nice" about it?]

This is true not only because flagrant boastfulness, vulgarity, immorality, and factiousness
are self-incriminating but also because they are
nation-corrupting. They move out from centers
of influence to infect whole cultures. The last
five years bear vivid witness to this infection at
almost every level of society. [John, take a trip to
the other side of the world. If a leader is perceived
as weak, other people will destroy that leader and
all those under them.]

This truth is not uniquely Christian: "A little leaven leavens the whole lump" (I Corinthians 5:6). "Bad company ruins good morals" (I Corinthians 15:33). Whether you embrace that company in your house or on social media, it corrupts. There are sins that "lead people into more and more ungodliness" as "their talk [spreads] like gangrene" (II Timothy 2:16–17).

There is a character connection between rulers and subjects. When the Bible describes a king by saying, "He sinned and made Israel to sin" (I Kings 14:16), it does not mean he twisted their arm. It means his influence shaped the people. That's the calling of a leader. Take the lead in giving shape to the character of your people. So it happens. For good or for ill.

Policies and Persons

Is it not baffling, then, that so many Christians seem to be sure that they are saving human lives and freedoms by treating as minimal the destructive effects of the spreading gangrene of high-profile, high-handed, culture-shaping sin? [John, it is becoming more and more evident that Trump has behaved better than Biden over the past four years.]

This point has a special relevance for Christians.

Freedom and life are precious. We all want to live and be free to pursue happiness. But if our freedoms, and even our lives, are threatened or taken, the essence of our identity in Christ, the certainty of our everlasting joy with Christ, and the holiness and love for which we have been saved by Christ—none of these is lost with the loss of life and freedom. [John, have you asked any aborted babies how they feel about this?]

Therefore, Christians communicate a falsehood to unbelievers (who are also baffled!) when we act as if policies and laws that protect life and freedom are more precious than being a certain kind of person. The church is paying dearly, and will continue to pay, for our communicating this falsehood year after year. [John, so "being nice" is the apex virtue? Show me a Bible verse.]

The justifications for ranking the destructive effects of persons below the destructive effects of policies ring hollow. [John, it depends on the level of power you give to the person versus the policy. If you really believe that, you would be supporting the self-government candidate versus the socialist.]

I find it bewildering that Christians can be so sure that greater damage will be done by bad judges, bad laws, and bad policies than is being done by the culture-infecting spread of the gangrene of sinful self-exaltation and boasting and strife-stirring (eristikos).

How do they know this? Seriously! Where do they get the sure knowledge that judges, laws, and policies are less destructive than boastful factiousness in high places? [John, you could look up abortion statistics. "Factiousness in high places?" You mean, like what Jesus did?]

What about Abortion?

Where does the wickedness of defending child-killing come from? It comes from hearts of self-absorbed arrogance and boasting (James 4:1–2). It comes from hearts that are insubordinate to God. In other words, it comes from the very character that so many Christian leaders are treating as comparatively innocuous because they think Roe and SCOTUS and Planned Parenthood are more pivotal, more decisive, battlegrounds.

I think Roe is an evil decision. I think Planned Parenthood is a code name for baby-killing and (historically at least) ethnic cleansing. And I think it is baffling and presumptuous to assume that proabortion policies kill more people than a culture-saturating, pro-self-pride. [Actually, communism has killed more people, John.]

When a leader models self-absorbed, self-exalting boastfulness, he models the most deadly behavior in the world. He points his nation to destruction. Destruction of more kinds than we can imagine. [Here Piper is virtue signaling bashing "toxic masculinity."]

It is naive to think that a man can be effectively pro-life and manifest consistently the character traits that lead to death—temporal and eternal. [Typical ad hominem: Piper tries to equate masculine character traits with evil.]

Word to Pastors

May I suggest to pastors that in the quietness of your study you do this? Imagine that America collapses. First anarchy, then tyranny—from the right or the left. [John, you know it's coming from the left. Stop it!] Imagine that religious freedom is gone. [John, Biden/Harris like to imagine that too!] What remains for Christians is fines, prison, exile, and martyrdom. [Thanks, John!] Then ask yourself this, "Has my preaching been developing real, radical Christians?" Christians who can sing on the scaffold,

> Let goods and kindred go,
> This mortal life also;
> The body they may kill: [or abort]
> God's truth abideth still;
> His kingdom is forever.

Christians who will act like the believers in Hebrews 10:34: "You joyfully accepted the plundering of your property, since you knew that you yourselves had a better possession and an abiding one." Christians who will face hate and reviling and exclusion for Christ's sake and yet "rejoice in that day, and leap for joy, for behold, [their] reward is great in heaven" (Luke 6:22–23).

Have you been cultivating real Christians who see the beauty and the worth of the Son of God? Have you faithfully unfolded and heralded "the unsearchable riches of Christ" (Ephesians 3:8)? Are you raising up generations of those who say with Paul, "I count everything as loss because of the surpassing worth of knowing Christ Jesus my Lord" (Philippians 3:8)?

Have you shown them that they are "sojourners and exiles" (I Peter 2:11), and that their "citizenship is in heaven," from which they "await a Savior, the Lord Jesus Christ" (Philippians 3:20)? Do they feel in their bones that "to live is Christ, and to die is gain" (Philippians 1:21)?

Or have you neglected these greatest of all realities and repeatedly diverted their attention onto the strategies of politics? Have you inadvertently created the mindset that the greatest issue in life is saving America and its earthly benefits? Or have you shown your people that the greatest issue is exalting Christ with or without America? Have you shown them that the people who do the most good for the greatest number for the longest time (including America!) are people who have the aroma of another world with another King?

Where does that leave me as I face a civic duty on November 3? Here's my answer. I do not require anyone to follow me (as if I could)—not my wife, not my friends, not my colleagues.

I will not develop some calculus to determine which path of destruction I will support. That is not my duty. My calling is to lead people to see Jesus Christ, trust his forgiveness for sins, treasure him above everything in this world, live in a way that shows his all-satisfying value, and help them make it to heaven with love and holiness. That calling is contradicted by supporting either pathway to cultural corruption and eternal ruin.

You may believe that there are kinds of support for such pathways that do not involve such a contradiction—such an undermining of authentic Christian witness. You must act on what you see. I can't see it. That is why I said my way need not be yours.

When I consider the remote possibility that I might do any good by endorsing the devastation already evident in the two choices before me, I am loath to undermine my calling (and the church's mission) to stand for Christ-exalting faith and hope and love.

I will be asked to give an account of my devotion to this life-giving calling. The world will ask. And the Lord of heaven will ask. And my conscience will ask. What will I say?

With a cheerful smile, I will explain to my unbelieving neighbor why my allegiance to Jesus set me at odds with death—death by abortion and death by arrogance. [John, this is one of the most arrogant articles published this year.] I will take him to Psalm 139 and Romans 1. And if he is willing, I will show him how abortion and arrogance can be forgiven because of Christ (Ephesians 1:7). And I will invite him to become an exile—to have a kingdom that will never be shaken, not even when America is a footnote [John, you seem to want this to happen] in the archives of the new creation.

On the Desiring God website (editor's note) after this article was published, John Piper tweeted, "The article we posted today explains why I won't be voting for Biden or Trump. That choice to 'write in' is relatively unimportant. But the reasoning really matters." He then linked to his 1995 article on abortion as a stake in the ground he hopes never to move.

What do these messages from these pastors have in common? They are trying to use the lie that there is something morally more important than abortion, and this mysterious new moral idea can be used to not only not support Trump but also to support Biden. I submit to you that these pastors are so feminized that they were completely put off by Trump's masculinity. So they had to go all in for the least masculine ticket and then rationalize their decision to the general public.

Keller and Dever? They have since been determined to be registered Democrats.

After all the Trump-bashing from the big-name pastors, they were joined by an ally. On August 23, 2020, Richard Spencer, the leading White supremacist in the US, endorsed Joe Biden.

Post-Election Analysis

We all know the results of the election and most of the subplots associated with it. Bloomberg published a demographic breakdown of donors to Trump or Biden by employer and occupation. [36]

The analysis shows that the NYPD, US Marines, and US Military were solidly behind Trump. These are also generally the most masculine organizations on the chart.

According to Bloomberg's analysis, the occupation that was most solidly behind Trump were homemakers, with stay-at-home moms close behind. These are the feminine women, then disabled people and people on disability. This demographic is more difficult to analyze, but it could possibly be masculine men who have injured themselves on the job. Then come welders, ranchers, HVAC professionals, truckers, plumbers, mechanics, electricians, construction workers, police officers, carpenters, and several other job descriptions that are usually associated with masculine men. My point is that Trump's most dedicated bases were men and women who believe in traditional gender roles. Ministers who donated went 47% to Trump and 53% to Biden. Evidently, many ministers were more concerned

---

[36] https://www.bloomberg.com/graphics/2020-election-trump-biden-donors/.

with "mean tweets" than projecting biblical beliefs, such as protecting the unborn, into the public sphere.

Defense Mechanisms of Trojan Horses

When a Trojan horse gets discovered or called out, you can expect one or more of the following responses from them or their apologists:

1) "Don't judge!"
2) "Everyone is a sinner."
3) "All sins are equal."
4) "The main thing we need to focus on is unity."
5) They will disavow the label while advocating the lie.

The Trojan horse will do whatever they can to stay inside the organization they are trying to destroy, and they also want to maintain their platform. According to Jon Harris, the Trojan horses will usually "deflect, deny, and disguise" to try to stay inside the gates. An example of this occurring was when some professors at Southern Seminary were exposed for teaching Critical Race Theory (more on this later in this book) in a positive light. Al Mohler, the president of Southern Seminary, in a Neville Chamberlain moment, then tweeted a picture of one of these professors signing the Abstract of Principles, the seminary's confession of faith.[37]

---

[37] "Deflect and Deny: Al Mohler and Thabiti Anyawbile Respond to Exposure of SBC Professors," 2018, https://enemieswithinthechurch.com/2019/09/04/deflect-and-deny-al-mohler-and-thabiti-anyawbile-respond-to-exposure-of-sbc-professors/.

CHAPTER 8

The Next Round—Direct Attacks on the Church

We have seen in previous chapters how the war on masculinity has negatively impacted the church. So while feminized churches are struggling with the deeper questions of the universe such as, "Does this pantsuit make me look fat?" far more sinister attacks against the church are underway.

In order to better understand what is happening in the church, let's look at the Personal Identity Matrix:

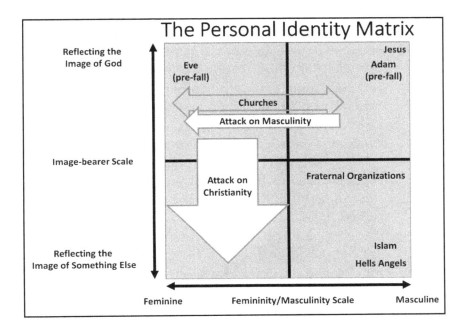

Once the church (or the average church) has been feminized by the attack on its masculinity, it is now set up for the next phases of the attack. Feminine (or matriarchal) organizations are not as good at defending themselves as the Masculine (or patriarchal) ones are.

Orginform

Richard Wurmbrand describes the structure of the Soviet effort to dismantle religion worldwide. The organization they have created is called Orginform. Here is a summary from Wurmbrand:

> A gigantic organism has been created by the Soviet Secret Police to destroy the churches in the whole world. Their first aim is to cancel or

minimize the hostility of religions toward communism. Additionally, they seek allies within the churches so they can use clerical prestige to bring the mass of believers into the camp of revolution. The name of this department is Orginform. It has secret cells in every country and in every large religious organization. One can assume that anti-Communist organizations and missions working behind the Iron Curtain are its main target. Communist agents specializing in propaganda and provocation infiltrate churches and missions to prepare the ideological disarmament of the faithful. Its first director, Vassilii Corclov, was formerly an Orthodox priest, an apostle turned Judas. The headquarters are in Warsaw. The actual leader is Theodor Krasky. Orginform has one school in Feodosia for training agents for Latin countries and one in Moscow for North America. The agents for Britain, Holland, Scandinavia, etc., are trained in Siguel (Latvia) and those for Moslem countries in Constantza (Romania). These schools prepare false pastors, priests, imams, and rabbis; each must understand thoroughly their respective theology. Some of them entrench themselves in churches or missions by posing as refugees. A Jesuit named Tondi, an Italian Communist, after attending the Lenin School in Moscow, was instructed by the Communist Party to enter a religious order; he became afterward a secretary to Pope Paul VI. His true role was discovered, and today, he openly declares himself to be a Communist and has married a comrade. He is still active in religious matters for the Communist Party and claims to have been forgiven by the Pope.[38]

The next time you see someone derided as a "conspiracy theorist," remember Orginform.

Bullying by Church Insurance Companies

I recently had a conversation with an assistant pastor at a small church. He told me that his church is insured for liability by a company that specializes in insuring churches. He also told me that the insurance company had written a condition (known as an exclusion rider) into their policy that if the church were sued by an LGBTQ activist group for saying anything the activist group found offensive, the insurance company would not cover the church. I am not aware of any pastors who have spoken out against this completely unfair bullying and leveraged religious discrimination by not only the LGBTQ community but also the insurance company.

Black Lives Matter and Antifa

Antifa and Black Lives Matter (BLM) are in the same section in this book because they often work together. In terms of property damage and the number of American citizens murdered, the combination of BLM and Antifa has done more damage to the United States than ISIS has.[39] BLM was founded by three women who have since admitted to being both trained Marxists and practicing witches. But because of the "new morality" that perceived underdogs are the source of moral truth as we will see in a future section, BLM now has effectively more moral authority in the United States than the pope. Even the name "Black Lives Matter" is designed to put all the

---

[38] Richard Wurmbrand, Marx and Satan, Westchester, Illinois, Crossway Books, p 100.

[39] https://merica1st.com/extremist-files/2020-blm-antifa-deaths/.

organization's opponents in "label jail." If you are not all in for BLM, you are labeled a racist.

Here are the original goals of BLM, according to their website [which has since been edited to a much weaker message]:

- The Black Lives Matter Global Network is as powerful as it is because of our membership, our partners, our supporters, our staff, and you. Our continued commitment to liberation for all Black people means we are continuing the work of our ancestors and fighting for our collective freedom because it is our duty.
- Every day, we recommit to healing ourselves and each other and to cocreating alongside comrades, allies, and family a culture where each person feels seen, heard, and supported.
- We acknowledge, respect, and celebrate differences and commonalities.
- We work vigorously for freedom and justice for Black people and, by extension, all people.
- We intentionally build and nurture a beloved community that is bonded together through a beautiful struggle that is restorative, not depleting.
- We are unapologetically Black in our positioning. In affirming that Black Lives Matter, we need not qualify our position. To love and desire freedom and justice for ourselves is a prerequisite for wanting the same for others.
- We see ourselves as part of the global Black family, and we are aware of the different ways we are impacted or privileged as Black people who exist in different parts of the world.
- We are guided by the fact that all Black lives matter, regardless of actual or perceived sexual

identity, gender identity, gender expression, economic status, ability, disability, religious beliefs or disbeliefs, immigration status, or location.

- We make space for transgender brothers and sisters to participate and lead.
- We are self-reflexive and do the work required to dismantle cisgender privilege and uplift Black trans folk, especially Black trans women who continue to be disproportionately impacted by trans-antagonistic violence.
- We build a space that affirms Black women and is free from sexism, misogyny, and environments in which men are centered.
- We practice empathy. We engage comrades with the intent to learn about and connect with their contexts.
- We make our spaces family-friendly and enable parents to fully participate with their children. We dismantle the patriarchal practice that requires mothers to work "double shifts" so that they can mother in private even as they participate in public justice work.
- We disrupt the Western-prescribed nuclear family structure requirement by supporting each other as extended families and "villages" that collectively care for one another, especially our children, to the degree that mothers, parents, and children are comfortable.
- We foster a queer-affirming network. When we gather, we do so with the intention of freeing ourselves from the tight grip of heteronormative thinking, or rather, the belief that all in the world are heterosexual (unless s/he or they disclose otherwise).

- We cultivate an intergenerational and communal network free from ageism. We believe that all people, regardless of age, show up with the capacity to lead and learn.
- We embody and practice justice, liberation, and peace in our engagements with one another.

Antifa stands for "anti-fascist." It's really a clever way to say "Marxist" or "Communist." When you look at the Political Identity Matrix, Antifa opposes everyone on the right (or hierarchical masculine) side. They lump Nazis and traditional conservative constitutionalists together as all being evil. It's an example of the "label jail" tactic we looked at earlier.

Direct Attack by BLM on Troy, New York, Church

People who are mad at God will eventually attack an image-bearer. Since the God-haters have been feminized, it will not usually be "lone wolf" attacks. The preferred method involves a "woke mob." Whom they attack will reveal the attacker's image of God. The attackers are trying to hurt God. The God-haters will rationalize their attacks by telling themselves they are "disrupting" patriarchy, systemic racism, homophobia, misogyny, etc. They will often try to "cancel" the victim or worse.

The level of hatred that Satan and his followers have for both Christianity and male masculinity was displayed on June 28, 2020, in Troy, New York.[40] Grace Baptist Church had announced an AR-15 giveaway. This was more than the local BLM leader, Lukee Forbes, could stand.[41] You really need to find some of the videos of the inci-

---

[40] "Disgusting: Black Lives Matter Mob Harasses and Attacks Church Members in Troy, New York," July 6, 2020, https://therightscoop.com/disgusting-black-lives-matter-mob-harasses-and-attacks-church-members-in-troy-new-york/.

[41] Tom Tillison, "BLM Protesters Who Stormed NY Church Services Were Led by City Employee with Violent Criminal Past, Reports Say," July 7, 2020, https://www.bizpacreview.com/2020/07/07/blm-protesters-who-stormed-ny-church-services-were-led-by-city-employee-with-violent-criminal-past-943863.

dent that are posted on the Internet. The depth of evil that you will see from the BLM activists is something you need to see with your own eyes. There are witches outside on the sidewalk trying to cast spells on the church, while BLM activists shout lies and swearwords at people who are walking into the church. Some of the people being heckled while walking into the church were small Black children.[42] All Black lives do not matter to BLM.

The Response—the Silence of the Lambs

The church has been feminized by the culture, infiltrated by Trojan Horses, and is now under direct attack on several fronts. Let's analyze the response.

Normalcy Bias

Before looking into the response of the church to these various external stimuli, let's study something called normalcy bias. Normalcy bias is described most succinctly by Wikipedia, "The normalcy bias, or normality bias, is a belief people hold when there is a possibility of a disaster. It causes people to underestimate both the likelihood of a disaster and its possible effects because people believe that things will always function the way things normally have functioned." About 70% of people respond with some form of normalcy bias when a disaster is unfolding.[43]

There are an estimated 52 million people who attend church in the United States on an average Sunday.[44] There are organized forces

---

[42] "Watch: BLM Activists Attack A Black Family As They Attempt To Enter Church In NYC," July 2020, https://en-volve.com/2020/07/06/watch-blm-activists-attack-a-black-family-as-they-attempt-to-enter-church-in-nyc/.

[43] Esther Inglis-Arkell, "The Frozen Calm of Normalcy Bias," May 2, 2013, https://io9.gizmodo.com/the-frozen-calm-of-normalcy-bias-486764924.

[44] Outreach Magazine, "7 Startling Facts: An Up Close Look at Church Attendance in America," May 4, 2018, https://churchleaders.com/pastors/pastor-articles/139575-7-startling-facts-an-up-close-look-at-church-attendance-in-america.html.

at work that intend to criminalize Christianity in the United States. Yet on the average Sunday morning, almost no church in America will even acknowledge the threat. The same highly leveraged bullying tactics used by the LGBTQ on US businesses are starting to be directed at churches.

Retreating to the Perceived Safety of a Personal Faith

Something you will notice when you listen to the primary message of most modern churches, Bible studies, or sermons is that it's all about…you! Part of the motive for this me, me, me message is the pressure to be "relevant" in a highly selfish culture. But part of it is the reluctance to engage the culture with truth because this will inevitably lead to conflict. Feminized churches have an extreme fear of conflict, so they focus on "safe" topics like personal faith and sanctification. There is absolutely nothing wrong with these topics unless things get totally out of balance, and they are. Even in some of the most "traditional-conservative" churches and denominations, the personal faith message gets played like a stuck record.

Small Groups

A somewhat recent trend in larger churches is to have small groups. Small groups can be a powerful ministry, especially in larger churches. But they can also degenerate into group therapy. If you look at what has been given up in order to move toward a small group model, one thing is the Wednesday night prayer meeting, and the other is evangelism. I can't help but wonder if we are now praying smaller because we meet smaller. In other words, the prayers that are happening in the small groups tend to be more self-centered than the prayers you would hear at a churchwide Wednesday night prayer meeting.

The Planned Kill Shot against Your Church

While we have seen the direct attack by BLM/Antifa on the church in Troy, New York, a more sinister and effective strategy for silencing your church is in the works. New Vice President Kamala Harris is a strong advocate of "marriage equality." The "marriage equality" advocates would like to soon force your church to agree to perform same-sex "marriages" or be severely penalized.

Let's revisit the chart we looked at earlier:

Sin	Form the person's identity	Externally signal the person's identity	Band together as a collective	Lobby for preferred civil rights status	Lobby to limit religious liberty	Try to force everyone to say their behavior is good	Try to punish anyone who does not believe like they do
Murder							
Adultery		•					
Fornication							
Lying							
Substance Abuse	•		•				
Stealing							
Homosexuality	•	•	•	•	•	•	•
Transgender	•	•	•	•	•	•	•

Table 15 Comparing sins

Notice the lower two rows in the chart. Those are the people who identify as LGBTQ. Also, notice the last three columns in the chart—"Lobby to limit religious liberty," "Try to force everyone to say their behavior is good," and "Try to punish anyone who does not believe like they do."

We see in the book of Amos, chapter 7, verses 10–13, an example of a pantheistic priest attempting to weaponize civil authority against Amos for "hate speech."

> Then Amaziah, the priest of Bethel, sent word to Jeroboam king of Israel, saying, "Amos has conspired against you in the midst of the house of

Israel; the land is unable to endure all his words. For thus Amos says, 'Jeroboam will die by the sword and Israel will certainly go from its land into exile.'" Then Amaziah said to Amos, "Go, you seer, flee away to the land of Judah and there eat bread and there do your prophesying! But no longer prophesy at Bethel, for it is a sanctuary of the king and a royal residence."

There is a bill in Congress right now (early 2021) called the "Equality Act" that will supposedly promote "equality" by modifying language in the 1964 Civil Rights Act, but the intent is something completely different.[45] The bill would have several devastating impacts on religious freedom.[46], [47]

1) Faith-based hospitals and insurers could be forced to provide gender-transition therapies that violate their religious beliefs.
2) Children could seek to change their gender without parental knowledge or consent.
3) Faith-based adoption and foster care agencies could be forced to place children with same-sex couples or lose their licenses.
4) The Act would dismantle sex-specific facilities, sports, and other spaces. As a result, biological females would be forced to compete in sports with biological males and for athletic scholar-

[45] Christopher Bedford, "'Blessings of Liberty:' How 'the Equality Act' Viciously Attacks Christians, Freedom, Society, Sex, and You," February 25, 2021, https://thefederalist.com/2021/02/25/blessings-of-liberty-how-the-equality-act-viciously-attacks-christians-freedom-society-sex-and-you/.

[46] Jim Dennison, "The Equality Act: What Christians need to know," February 26, 2021, https://www.denisonforum.org/resources/the-equality-act-what-christians-need-to-know/.

[47] Tony Perkins, "Equality Act Assails Religious Freedom," April 1, 2021, https://www.frc.org/get.cfm?i=PV21D04.

ships. Sexual assaults on girls in bathrooms and showers could escalate.

5) Faith-based schools and businesses could be forced to violate their beliefs regarding homosexual activity and LGBTQ behavior or face fines, censure, or worse.

6) Churches that rent their facilities to the public could be forced to rent them for same-sex marriages and other LGBTQ events.

Despite their "nice" veneer, the LGBTQ community seems to have a persistent effort to weaponize civil government against the church, just like in the book of Amos. Instead of building their own church, they want to change yours. And if you do not change your church the way they want you to, they want to punish you.

CHAPTER 9

Moving Organizations around the Political Identity Matrix

Before the totalitarian/egalitarian false utopia can be built, the current order must be destroyed. Here is what the endgame for the totalitarian/egalitarians looks like:

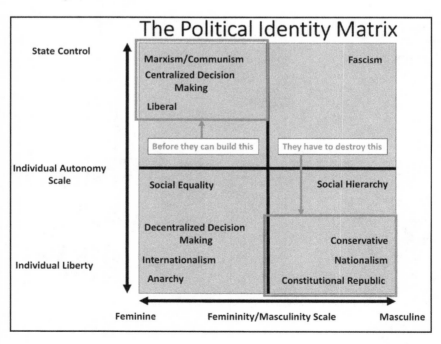

The above chart shows that any limits to centralized authority have to be destroyed before Satan's endgame can be built. The Constitutional Republic that was invented and developed in the United States is the largest obstacle to worldwide tyranny and therefore is the biggest target.

How to Destroy a System

There are several common ways to destroy a system, whether it is the human body, a machine, or an organization. Here is a list of the most common ones, divided by personal and organizational:

Personal

1) Operate the system in a way for which it was not designed
2) Hinder the system's ability to repair itself

Organizational

1) Feminize the organization
2) "Immoralize" the organization
3) Demoralize the organization
4) Divide the organization against itself
5) Inject chaos into the system (replace law and order with lawlessness and disorder; you can see BLM and Antifa do this on a regular basis)
6) Attack the organization with a Trojan horse
7) Decapitate the system

Unfortunately, if you are paying attention, you can see many of these forces in play in our world today. Let's dig deeper and look at some destructive forces that are currently at work.

Hegelian Dialectic—Destroying the Current Order

A classic military strategy is "divide and conquer," where you attempt to divide your enemy in some way. Then you can fight a much smaller enemy. It's even more effective if once you divide your enemy, you can pit the two sides against each other. The strategy that Marxism uses to accomplish this is known as the Hegelian dialectic.

Marxism sets up binary conflicts between identity groups. Matthew 12:25 states, "And knowing their thoughts Jesus said to them, 'Any kingdom divided against itself is laid waste; and any city or house divided against itself will not stand.'" So if you can motivate an organization to divide against itself, you will cause it to destroy itself. Any movement or action such as Social Justice that seeks to split the United States into two groups—"oppressor" or "oppressed"—is following the classic Marxism playbook to divide and destroy the United States, or at least the current order in the United States.

Marxism has historically created two opposing groups—"proletariat" versus "bourgeoisie," "workers" versus "nonworkers," "oppressed" versus "oppressor." Identifying one group as a "victim group" gives the "victim group" two things. One is a reason to fight the other group, and the other is a moral rationalization for fighting them. It basically tricks the "victim group" into doing something evil by making them think they are doing something good.

The Hegelian dialectic takes advantage of one of the feminine traits that "peace" is more important than truth. What ends up happening is a "compromise loop." Keep in mind that the Marxists will start a conflict with the objective of "moving the needle" on the current order into disorder. Here is an example of how they have been doing this. What happens is an antithesis is publicized throughout the culture to attack the thesis. In order to relieve the tension, the culture adopts the synthesis.

Here is round one:

Thesis	Anithesis	Synthesis
First Way	Second Way	"Third Way"
Individualism	Collectivism	Individual "ownership" with state control
Capitalism	Communism	Communitarianism
Christianity	Marxism	Liberation Theology
Nationalism	Globalism	European Union
Creation	Evolution	Theistic Evolution
Theism	Atheism	New Age
Good	Evil	Moral Relativism

Table 16 Hegelian process, round one

Round two happens when the Marxists punish the "niceness" of their opponents by continuing to push. With the mainstream media assisting, people eventually burn out on the conflict and give in. Here is what happens:

Thesis	Anithesis	Synthesis
"Third Way"	Second Way	Second Way
Individual "ownership" with state control	Collectivism	Collectivism
Communitarianism	Communism	Communism
Liberation Theology	Marxism	Marxism
European Union	Globalism	Globalism
Theistic Evolution	Evolution	Evolution
New Age	Atheism	One World Religion
Moral Relativism	Evil	Evil "re-branded" as good

Table 17. Hegelian process, round two.

Here is really what is happening. You can see the ridiculous "logic" that is applied to cause chaos in the current order:

Thesis	Anithesis	Synthesis
Truth	Error	Error
2+2=4	2+2<>4	2+2=5

Table 18. Hegelian process creating lies and chaos.

There is only one response to the Hegelian dialectic—never give an inch.

The Road Map—The Communist Manifesto

According to laissez-fairerepublic.com,[48] here is an analysis of the ten planks of the Communist Manifesto and how they have been implemented in the United States:

1. Abolition of private property in land and application of all rents of land to public purpose

   The courts have interpreted the 14th amendment of the US Constitution (1868) to give the government far more "eminent domain" power than was originally intended. Under the rubric of "eminent domain" and various zoning regulations, land use regulations by the Bureau of Land Management, property taxes, and "environmental" excuses, private property rights have become very diluted and private property in lands, vehicles, and other forms are seized almost every day in this country under the "forfeiture" provisions of the RICO statutes and the so-called War on Drugs.

---

[48] http://www.laissez-fairerepublic.com/TenPlanks.html.

2. A heavy progressive or graduated income tax

   The 16th amendment of the US Constitution, 1913 (which some scholars maintain was never properly ratified), and various state income taxes established this major Marxist coup in the United States many decades ago. These taxes continue to drain the lifeblood out of the American economy and greatly reduce the accumulation of desperately needed capital for future growth, business starts, job creation, and salary increases.

3. Abolition of all rights of inheritance

   Another Marxian attack on private property rights is in the form of federal and state estate taxes and other inheritance taxes, which have abolished or at least greatly diluted the right of private property owners to determine the disposition and distribution of their estates upon their death. Instead, government bureaucrats get their greedy hands involved.

4. Confiscation of the property of all emigrants and rebels

   We call it government seizures, tax liens, "forfeiture" Public "law" 99-570 (1986); Executive order 11490, sections 1205, 2002 which gives private land to the Department of Urban Development; the imprisonment of "terrorists" and those who speak out or write against the "government" (1997 Crime/Terrorist Bill); or the IRS confiscation of property without due process.

5. Centralization of credit in the hands of the state by means of a national bank with state capital and an exclusive monopoly

The Federal Reserve System, created by the Federal Reserve Act of Congress in 1913, is indeed such a "national bank," and it politically manipulates interest rates and holds a monopoly on legal counterfeiting in the United States. This is exactly what Marx had in mind and completely fulfills this plank, another major socialist objective. Yet most Americans naively believe the US of A is far from a Marxist or socialist nation.

6. Centralization of the means of communication and transportation in the hands of the state

In the US, communication and transportation are controlled and regulated by the Federal Communications Commission (FCC) established by the Communications Act of 1934 and the Department of Transportation and the Interstate Commerce Commission (established by Congress in 1887) and the Federal Aviation Administration as well as Executive orders 11490, 10999—not to mention various state bureaucracies and regulations. There is also the federal postal monopoly, AMTRAK and CONRAIL—outright socialist (government-owned) enterprises. Instead of free-market private enterprise in these important industries, these fields in America are semi-cartelized through the government's regulatory-industrial complex.

7. Extension of factories and instruments of pro-
    duction owned by the state, the bringing into
    cultivation of wastelands, and the improvement
    of the soil generally in accordance with a com-
    mon plan

    While the US does not have vast "collective
    farms" (which failed so miserably in the Soviet
    Union), we nevertheless do have a significant
    degree of government involvement in agriculture
    in the form of price support subsidies and acre-
    age allotments and land-use controls. The Desert
    Entry Act and The Department of Agriculture, as
    well as the Department of Commerce and Labor,
    Department of Interior, the Environmental
    Protection Agency, Bureau of Land Management,
    Bureau of Reclamation, Bureau of Mines,
    National Park Service, and the IRS control of
    business through corporate regulations.

8. Equal obligation of all to work, establishment of
    Industrial armies, especially for agriculture

    We call it the Social Security Administration and
    the Department of Labor. The National debt
    and inflation caused by the communal bank
    has caused the need for a two "income" family.
    Women in the workplace since the 1920s, the
    nineteenth amendment of the US Constitution,
    the Civil Rights Act of 1964, assorted Socialist
    Unions, affirmative action, the Federal Public
    Works Program, and, of course, Executive order
    11000. And I almost forgot…the Equal Rights
    Amendment means that women should do all
    work that men do, including the military and

since passage it would make women subject to the draft.

9. Combination of agriculture with manufacturing industries, gradual abolition of the distinction between town and country by a more equable distribution of the population over the country

   We call it the Planning Reorganization Act of 1949, zoning (Title 17 1910–1990) and Super Corporate Farms, as well as Executive orders 11647, 11731 (ten regions) and Public "law" 89-136.

10. Free education for all children in government schools, abolition of children's factory labor in its present form, combination of education with industrial production, etc.

    People are being taxed to support what we call "public" schools, which train the young to work for the communal debt system. We also call it the Department of Education, the NEA, and Outcome-Based "Education."

You can see that despite their evil agenda being published for all to see, the Marxists/communists/totalitarians have had significant success in implementing much of it already.

The Tricky RINOs

A mere forty-five days after the September 11, 2001, terror-ist attacks, in a wave of panicked patriotism, Congress passed, and George W. Bush signed into law, the Patriot Act. In June of 2013, Edward Snowden revealed that the United States was using the

Patriot Act to spy more on its own citizens than on any terrorist group. This revelation revealed that a massive move to totalitarianism had occurred under a supposedly conservative president. Bush is sometimes called a RINO (Republican in Name Only), and the Patriot Act was a microcosm of what has been happening for decades as the United States has trended toward totalitarianism. In an effort to legislate security, Americans have traded off freedom. The Political Matrix below shows what commonly happens:

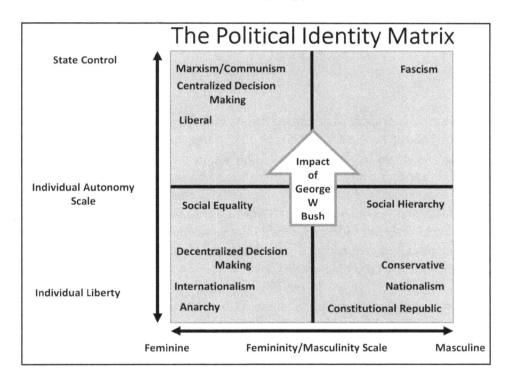

The lesson is that when our politicians decide to get "tough on terror," "tough on our enemies," or "tough on crime," look out because what they are most likely about to get tough on is your freedom.

CHAPTER 10

Cultural Marxism—
Weaponized Group Identity

Classical Marxism, as described earlier, had a big problem in the West, particularly in the United States. The large middle class prevented Marxists from using their usual "rich versus poor" Hegelian dialectic to divide and conquer the United States. They had to come up with another strategy. That strategy was to divide the United States by race. This strategy is called Cultural Marxism. This strategy is also known as Identity Politics.[49] Identity would now be weaponized to try to destroy a capitalist constitutional republic—the United States. Cultural Marxism is a false binary like Classical Marxism. The goal is to create "have" cultures versus "have-not" cultures. You will notice a visible connection between Marxism and Cultural Marxism at any Marxist, Antifa, or BLM march. It's the clenched fist salute. Historically, the identity group that considers itself the "have-not" group will use the clenched fist salute to symbolize a fight against authority. Cultural Marxism has an additional advantage that anyone who opposes it can be falsely labeled a racist. The Cultural Marxists, like the Classical Marxists, have created the same false binary that makes for a good fight. Ultimately, everyone is forced to choose whether they are an "anti-racist" (the new clever description for a Marxist) or a racist. Let's

---

[49] P. Andrew Sandlin, "Cultural Marxism, Simply Explained," April 23, 2018, https://docsandlin.com/2018/04/23/cultural-marxism-simply-explained/.

revisit the chart we have seen earlier showing what Marxists want to destroy and what they want to build in its place:

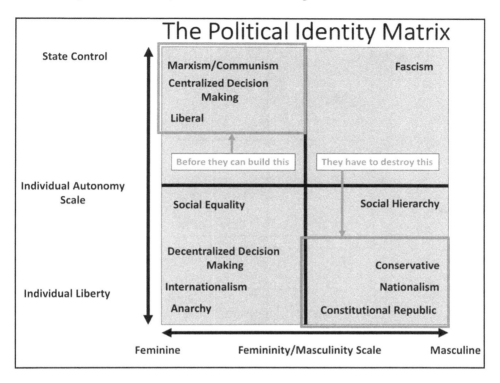

In order for Cultural Marxism to work, a couple of things needed to happen. The first was that the optics would be better if the middle class could be at least partially stratified into the upper and lower classes. This is why for decades, there has been a war on the middle class in the United States. This was the same goal that Classical Marxism had. But there was a more important shift that had to occur. The culture as a whole and the men, in particular, had to be feminized. A feminized culture struggles with individual achievement. They don't know how to create wealth outside of an organization. Feminized people are not comfortable having to figure out what to do. They have a strong "herding" instinct. Masculine people do not enjoy celebrating their own victimhood. But this is exactly the set of conditions that Cultural Marxism needs in order to accomplish its endgame, which is cultural destruction.

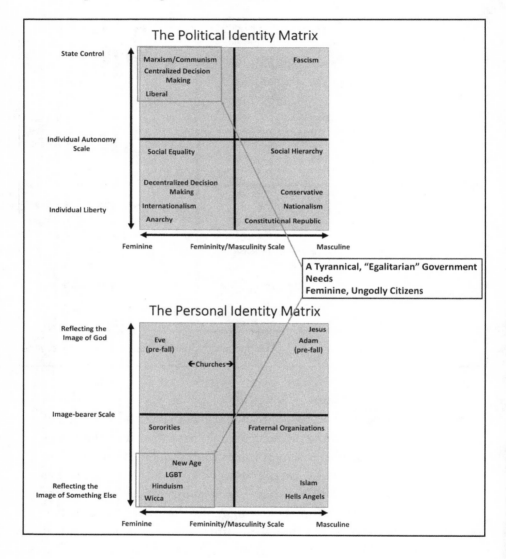

As seen above, a tyrannical government needs feminized, ungodly citizens. But feminized, ungodly citizens also need a tyrannical government. The cultural shifts on the Personal Identity Matrix have set up a tension on Political Identity Matrix. The tension is relieved through a move to the upper left.

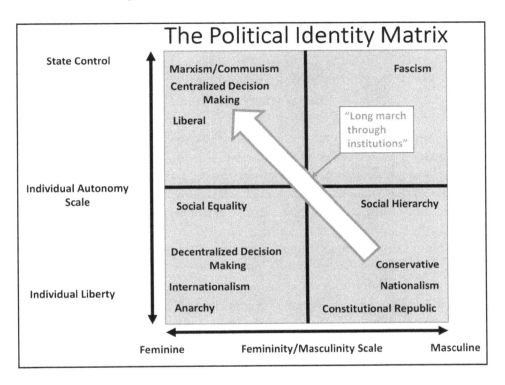

Cultural Marxists constantly talk about "systemic racism." Even though you can get a four-year degree in systems engineering, Cultural Marxists struggle to produce a flow chart of the "system" so that the racism in the system can be analyzed. What they do produce are even more forced binaries. Sandlin explains, "Cultural Marxists portray one pole of the binary (women, homosexuals, millennials, blacks) as oppressed and demand that the state liberate them from their oppressors. Oppression here almost never means literal enslavement, abuse, or assault. Rather, it means disrespect, disapproval, or social inequality. If, for example, homosexuals are not as respected as heterosexuals, they are oppressed and deserve state-coerced liberation. This is also where the new campus speech codes come from. The newly defined oppressed (millennials) are entitled not to be offended by words from the oppressing class (older Whites, teachers, men)."[50]

Cultural Marxism has the same horrible endgame as Classical Marxism, which is totalitarian control by the Marxists. Always try to figure out what the endgame is.

Social Justice
The Counterfeit Gospel

In the last chapter, we looked at how to destroy a system. We primarily looked at politics. Now we will look at how to destroy a religion and, in the course of destroying a religion, create a new religion that will destroy the overall culture. Some people would consider Social Justice in the church to be a Trojan horse. Unfortunately, I think it is just too big to be considered a Trojan horse or at least is so big it needs to be looked at separately.

If Cultural Marxism is a political system, it has given birth to a new religion called Social Justice. Once you understand that Critical Race Theory, Woke Theology, and Liberation Theology are all "denominations" of this new religion, the way it is starting to appear in different kinds of organizations, such as churches, schools, and corporations, will make more sense to you.

---

[50] P. Andrew Sandlin, "Cultural Marxism, Simply Explained," April 23, 2018, https://docsandlin.com/2018/04/23/cultural-marxism-simply-explained/.

The endgame of the new Social Justice religion is to facilitate the desired move we previously looked at on the Political Identity Matrix:

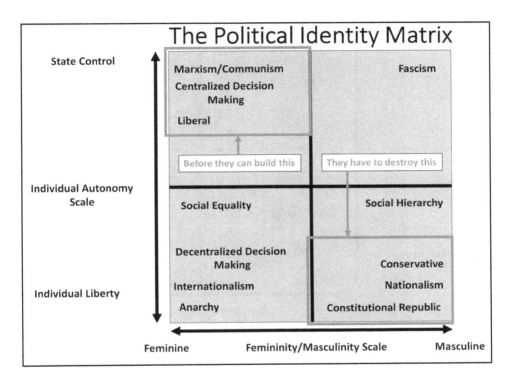

By making it a matter of moral imperative:

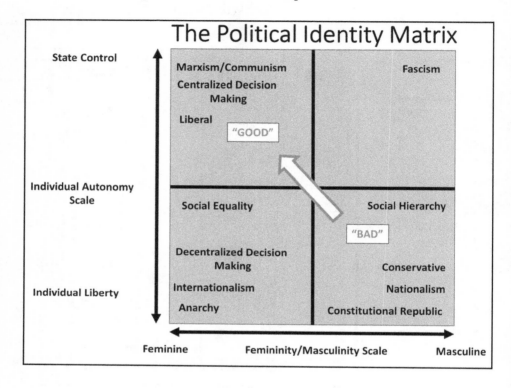

The Social Justice advocates have made things intentionally complicated, so it helps if you start by looking at their endgame. Christopher Rufo writes in *Imprimis*, "According to [SJ Leader Ibram] Kendi, 'In order to truly be antiracist, you also have to truly be anti-capitalist.' In other words, identity is the means, and Marxism is the end."[51]

One of the "denominations" of the new Social Justice religion is Critical Race Theory. Here are its core beliefs:

1) You are identified as a member of a group, not as an individual.

---

[51] Christopher Rufo, "Critical Race Theory: What It Is and How to Fight It," March 2021, https://imprimis.hillsdale.edu/critical-race-theory-fight/.

2) There are two groups of people, and you are either in the "oppressor" group or the "oppressed" group.
3) Your fundamental duty is freeing groups from oppression.
4) Lived experience is more important than objective evidence in understanding oppression.
5) People from "oppressed" groups have special insight into truth that is fundamentally inaccessible to "oppressor" groups. (Does this include Candace Owens?)

Notice how most theories have a scientific statement of cause and effect, but CRT reads like a religion right from the start. The unwritten and unspoken foundational assumption of the current iterations of Social Justice, Critical Race Theory, Woke Theology, and Liberation Theology is that Black people are a failed race. If you don't believe me, start with the assumption that "Black people are a highly successful and accomplished race" and try to build the CRT beliefs on that foundation and see how it works. No, CRT is not coming from the Ku Klux Klan. This is foundational to what is being taught at most major universities.

Jon Harris has done a great job of researching the Social Justice belief system. Here are some of his findings:

How Social Justice Parallels the Gospel	
White / Male / Straight Privilege	Original Sin
Political Correctness	The Law
Woke	Born Again
Liberal Politics	Sacraments
Woke Leaders	Priests
Sociology	Canon
Equality	Heaven

Table 19. Religious traits of Social Justice.

I will add another: canceling someone parallels excommunication. Here is a chart Harris put together that shows the conversion process of the new Social Justice religion:

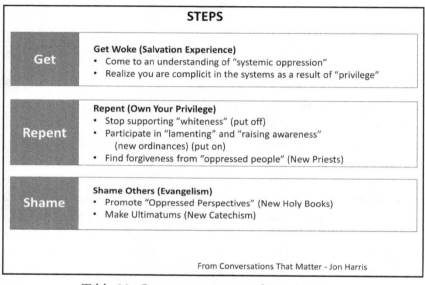

STEPS	
Get	**Get Woke (Salvation Experience)** • Come to an understanding of "systemic oppression" • Realize you are complicit in the systems as a result of "privilege"
Repent	**Repent (Own Your Privilege)** • Stop supporting "whiteness" (put off) • Participate in "lamenting" and "raising awareness" (new ordinances) (put on) • Find forgiveness from "oppressed people" (New Priests)
Shame	**Shame Others (Evangelism)** • Promote "Oppressed Perspectives" (New Holy Books) • Make Ultimatums (New Catechism)
	From Conversations That Matter - Jon Harris

Table 20. Conversion process of Social Justice.

He also points out some Biblical problems with Social Justice:

1) Merging law with grace creates a "different gospel."
2) Liberation Theology (and CRT) include a different gospel (false gospel), a different ethic (pharisaic), and a belief in subjective truth (gnostic).
3) Evangelicals who adopt aspects of Liberation Theology adopt one or more of these categories.
4) The secular Social Justice movement is a false religion.
5) Scripture warns against false teaching/teachers.

Here are some other objections to the new Social Justice / Woke / CRT Theology:

1) All humans are made in the image of God.
2) Only some people can be racist (White). Others cannot.
3) Leviticus 19:15 says, "'You shall do no injustice in judgment; you shall not be partial to the poor nor defer to the great, but you are to judge your neighbor fairly."
4) CRT really hurts Black people. It has done nothing to help. Imagine if all these resources wasted on CRT were actually used to fund scholarships for Black children.
5) CRT convinces people that they have no ability to create their own success. Their success or failure is defined by which group they are a part of.
6) Unequal weights and measures are outlawed in the Bible.
7) CRT is a forced binary. It tries to take something complicated and make it binary.
8) "Rise up" really means "tear down."
9) The counterfeit gospel of Social Justice does not care about evangelism to Black people or anyone else.
10) Numbers don't make you an oppressor; bad behavior does.
11) SJ is always trying to link slavery to all Christianity.
12) Racism/slavery is the unforgivable and only sin.
13) Guilt is only by association. There is little individual accountability.
14) White Christians were the primary agents in abolishing slavery.
15) There is a constant effort to link "White Supremacy" and Christianity.
16) SJ tries to transmit guilt through space and time simply by using skin color.
17) The Old Testament has laws about not punishing children for the sins of their fathers.
18) Social Justice supports intergenerational vengeance and unforgiveness.

19) SJ completely ignores Black Christians in Africa who are being oppressed by Muslims.
20) There is a constant changing of the Bible or words in the Bible. The theory and narrative always come first.
21) This one is surprising to the naive, but there is zero intent on forgiveness or reconciliation by most of the people who follow SJ.
22) What is the endgame of each of these belief systems? Social Justice theology clearly states that there is not a state where "the work is done," but in reality, the "work will be done" when the current order is destroyed.

Here are some scriptures that contradict the counterfeit gospel of SJ/CRT:

> But avoid foolish controversies and genealogies and strife and disputes about the Law, for they are unprofitable and worthless. Reject a factious man after a first and second warning, knowing that such a man is perverted and is sinning, being self-condemned. (Titus 3:9–11)

> The person who sins will die. A son will not suffer the punishment for the father's guilt, nor will a father suffer the punishment for the son's guilt; the righteousness of the righteous will be upon himself, and the wickedness of the wicked will be upon himself. (Ezekiel 18:20)

> Now we command you, brethren, in the name of our Lord Jesus Christ, that you keep away from every brother who leads an unruly life and not according to the tradition which you received from us. (II Thessalonians 3:6)

Many people, including many gullible Christians, have hopped on the "woke" bus without having any idea of where it is going. Effeminate (a.k.a. feminized) men are surprisingly comfortable operating within a mob. The endgame of Social Justice is to divide by oppressor or oppressed groups, build a case that the current system is so filled with "whiteness," "systemic racism," or some other label that the only option is to destroy the current order. So the "bait" of the new religion of Social Justice is that it will provide harmonious reconciliation between the races, but the "switch" is that it is really designed to divide Black and White people, destroy the current order, and ultimately increase the level of oppression of all races.

Comparing and Contrasting the Messages

Let's look at the Trojan horse of Social Justice / Critical Race Theory / Woke Theology. It's important when analyzing false belief systems to measure what they are emphasizing. For a baseline, here is the entire book of Acts analyzed by a word frequency counter:

Keyword	Frequency
all	173
God	163
when	115
Lord	107
men	95
came	87
man	83
also	75
one	73
Jesus	72

Table 21. Keyword count in Acts.

It makes a little more sense when analyzed by the numbers of two-word phrases:

Keyword (x2)	Frequency
Holy Spirit	41
Lord Jesus	19
Jesus Christ	18
next day	17
when heard	11
name Jesus	11

Table 22. Keyword count in Acts (two words).

For comparison and contrast, I put the last two articles from CRT/Woke thought leader Jemar Tisby into a word counter. Here is what it looks like:

Keyword	Frequency
White	20
Race	17
Rights	17
Evangelicals	14
Black	14

Table 23. Keyword count—Jemar Tisby.

I have sampled enough "Woke Theology" tweets, articles, and blogs to know that this is a pretty representative sample. They would all have similar word distribution and would show the same stark contrast with the book of Acts.

It's obvious that the book of Acts is concerned with someone's "spiritual DNA," while Tisby's writing is more concerned with someone's physical DNA. This is probably a rather good definition of racism. "Hate coaches," like Tisby, make Martin Luther King sound like Rush Limbaugh.

Are you more concerned with getting points with the "woke crowd" or in genuinely helping Black people? It may surprise you that these two choices are in diametric opposition.

Here is a summary from Jon Harris of some major contrasts between Social Justice Theology and the Gospel:

How Social Justice Contradicts the Gospel	
Focus:	External Behaviors Instead of a Heart Condition
Group:	Oppressor Classes Instead of Individuals
Order:	Sanctification Precedes Justification
Power:	Perpetual Repentance Instead of Justification

Table 24. How Social Justice contradicts the Gospel.

A constant mantra from Social Justice advocates is that the past is bad, and the Social Justice advocates don't present much of a vision for the future. Like the Marxists that they are, they do not want you to be able to use the past to reconstruct the current order. So the Social Justice advocates are abusing theology to morally judge the past and therefore completely erase it. But for now, the real war is in the present.

The real danger of these false belief systems is that the formerly mainstream church is now adopting some of them. Social Justice presents itself as a bolt-on or new "lens" you can use to see new "truth" to emphasize in scripture. But, as usual, what happens is that the new "lens" becomes the core belief system, and the totality of the Bible becomes secondary. This leads to a weakened and imbalanced church. A good example is what used to be a strength of the church and Christianity: the ability to define what is right and wrong. Even though we now have a culture that is obsessed with lawlessness, our culture is now quite forcefully defining right and wrong based on a hierarchy of perceived victimhood. When this "hierarchy of per-ceived victimhood" is also used to determine who "deserves" to be in power, we are ending up with a lot of evil, incompetent people in power. Power plus evil is a tragic combination.

Since 1973, over 61 million babies have been murdered in the United States due to abortion. Many of these babies are Black. But the Social Justice / CRT / Woke crowd is completely silent on this issue.

CRT is promoted as providing racial reconciliation but, in reality, divides by culture and does not help Black people now nor in the end. Black identity religions are growing more segregationist as the White churches are under pressure to integrate more. This is a recipe for failure and frustration. We will look at some of these identity-based religions in a future chapter.

Social Justice in the Workplace: Marginalizing Christians and Men

Since Social Justice is essentially a new religion, major corporations are currently engaged in a virtue-signaling exercise to show others how "woke" they are. (I have heard Virtue Signaling defined as "offending those who cannot harm them to appease those who can.") For all the talk about diversity, it has finally become obvious that "woke" corporations want people who look different but who think exactly the same. In other words, they want near-zero thought diversity. This means that eventually, these large corporations will have to engage in "thought policing" exercises to root out and fire (cancel) anyone who does not have the same Social Justice (hence, religious) values that they have. Imagine that the major corporation that you may own stock in could be practicing church discipline more effectively than the average church does.

Critical Race Theory and "Woke" Training

These training classes are the "sermons" of the new religion. Some companies have already started Critical Race Theory training where they pay Marxists (often from a local college or university) to have training classes where employees are either "converted," flagged as having "White fragility," or are labeled as "racist" and fired. There are probably a few minor "White fragility" cases found at every seminar. That way, the "woke coach" can come back (there is always "more work to be done") and charge for another seminar so that people can continue to repent of their "whiteness." Keep in mind that all the money spent on these seminars could have been spent on actually helping the Black (or other "marginalized") communities through something like the United Way. But that's not really the endgame, is it? The "woke" Cultural Marxists have a utopian endgame that is far more important to them than actually helping poor people.

Diversity, Equity, and Inclusion (DEI)

Let's look at some of the weapons that have been deployed against what I would call godly masculinity. There was a time when it was clearly unacceptable for any of us to be identified in the lower quadrants on the Personal Identity Matrix. Satan and those doing his work had to start off with a public relations campaign, if you will, to make it acceptable for men to move into the lower left quadrant and for women to move into the lower right quadrant. The first tactic was a war of ideas. And probably the first idea you started hearing about was the concept of tolerance. Tolerance was defined as "all viewpoints are equally valid." But notice that as the culture has changed, you don't hear the mantra anymore that "all viewpoints are equally valid," at least you don't hear it being applied to Christianity. "All viewpoints are equally valid" is quite the opposite of Jesus being the only way to heaven. Classical tolerance means being civil toward someone you disagree with. It's actually impossible to exercise tolerance toward someone you agree with.

The other weapon in this war of ideas is what you will hear described as diversity and inclusion. "Diversity and inclusion" are now only applied to the men in the lower left quadrant or women in the lower right quadrant. You will never hear an organization say that they are trying to increase the number of masculine Christian men or straight Christian women in that organization. All the "diversity and inclusion" efforts have had the opposite effect. You can look on the

Identity Matrix and see that if we had true diversity and inclusion, you'd see a scattering of these various people and groups in an organization. We now see a very deliberate effort to promote the lower left quadrant. One of the taglines you'll hear in the effort to promote this lower left quadrant is "everyone should be comfortable bringing their true self (or their authentic self) to work." But what if your "true self" is that you are a straight Christian masculine male? What if your "true self" is a nudist? Or maybe a better example is that every workplace mass shooter brought their true self to work that day.

There is also a danger of giving people power primarily based on a false identity of their belonging to a "victim group." This is by definition a form of discrimination, and we should not be surprised when discrimination leads to more discrimination. Once someone from a "victim group" is put in power, it is natural for them to discriminate against anyone who is not one of "their people." It would also be hypocritical for the discriminating organization to not allow its employees or members to discriminate based on the same identity-based "victim group" system.

Feminized organizations have pushed aside their mission, vision, and principles in order to build a playground of "inclusion." Don't be surprised when vitally important organizations such as the US Navy start to look and perform like "The Good Ship Lollipop."

The Corporate Equality Index

In the early stages of the culture war, we were told that what we did in our bedrooms and with whom was our business and nobody else's. Nowadays, you will probably find that the company you work for deeply cares about what you are doing in your bedroom. And if it's not heterosexual monogamous sex, they want to promote you for it. There is now an unofficial virtue-signaling contest on social media where each large company tries to outdo the others by hyping their efforts to promote anyone except straight White males.

One of the primary tactics being used is the Corporate Equality Index.

The Corporate Equality Index is essentially a social credit score for big corporations. Here is the most recent iteration:

Rating Criteria for the 2020 CEI

1. Workforce Protections (30 points possible)

    - Policy includes sexual orientation for all operations (15)
    - Policy includes gender identity or expression for all operations (15)

2. Inclusive Benefits (30 points possible)

    To secure full credit for benefits criteria, each benefit must be available to all benefits-eligible US employees. In areas where more than one health insurance plan is available, at least one inclusive plan must be available.

    - Equivalency in same—and different-sex spousal medical and soft benefits (10)
    - Equivalency in same—and different-sex domestic partner medical and soft benefits (10)
    - Equal health coverage for transgender individuals without exclusion for medically necessary care (10) (more info)

3. Supporting an inclusive culture & corporate social responsibility (40 points possible)

    a. Three LGBTQ internal training and education best practices (10)

- Businesses must demonstrate a firm-wide, sustained, and accountable commitment to diversity and cultural competency, including at least three of the following elements:

  o New hire training clearly states that the nondiscrimination policy includes gender identity and sexual orientation and provides definitions or scenarios illustrating the policy for each

  o Supervisors undergo training that includes gender identity and sexual orientation as discrete topics (maybe part of a broader training) and provides definitions or scenarios illustrating the policy for each

  o Integration of gender identity and sexual orientation in professional development, skills-based, or other leadership training that includes elements of diversity and/or cultural competency

  o Gender transition guidelines with supportive restroom, dress code, and documentation guidance

  o Anonymous employee engagement or climate surveys conducted on an annual or biennial basis allow employees the option to identify as LGBTQ

  o Data collection forms that include employee race, ethnicity, gender, military and disability status—typically recorded as part of employee records—include optional questions on sexual orientation and gender identity.

○ Senior management/executive performance measures include LGBTQ diversity metrics

b. Employee group or diversity council (10)
c. Three distinct efforts of outreach or engagement to broader LGBTQ community (15)

- Businesses must demonstrate ongoing LGBTQ-specific engagement that extends across the firm, including at least three of the following:

  ○ LGBTQ employee recruitment efforts with a demonstrated reach of LGBTQ applicants (required documentation may include a short summary of the event or an estimation of the number of candidates reached)
  ○ Supplier diversity program with demonstrated effort to include certified LGBTQ suppliers
  ○ Marketing or advertising to LGBTQ consumers (e.g., advertising with LGBTQ content, advertising in LGBTQ media, or sponsoring LGBTQ organizations and events)
  ○ Philanthropic support of at least one LGBTQ organization or event

(e.g., financial, in-kind or pro bono support)

- ○ Demonstrated public support for LGBTQ equality under the law through local, state, or federal legislation or initiatives

d. LGBTQ corporate social responsibility

- • Contractor/supplier nondiscrimination standards and philanthropic giving guidelines (5)

4. Responsible citizenship (-25)

Employers will have 25 points deducted from their score for a large-scale official or public anti-LGBTQ blemish on their recent records. Scores on this criterion are based on information that has come to HRC's attention related to topics including but not limited to undue influence by a significant shareholder calculated to undermine a business's employment policies or practices related to its LGBTQ employees, directing corporate charitable contributions to organizations whose primary mission includes advocacy against LGBTQ equality, opposing shareholder resolutions reasonably aimed at encouraging the adoption of inclusive workplace policies, revoking inclusive LGBTQ policies or practices, or engaging in proven practices that are contrary to the business's written LGBTQ employment policies.

Point Allocations

> Businesses are rated on a scale from 0 to 100, with a certain number of points awarded for meeting each criterion. The HRC Foundation will continue to award partial credit to employers that have satisfied a portion of certain criterion.[52]

This is highly leveraged bullying. It's also the opposite of diversity and inclusion since there is zero allowance for thought diversity or religious diversity. This will have the impact of moving Christians out of the workplace, which will defund our churches. Maybe the likelihood of decreasing tithe money will wake up some of our pastors.

To illustrate the inconsistency of the CEI, let's look at Rachel Dolezal. Yes, you probably remember her, the NAACP activist who was discovered to be White. Let's look physically at who she is. The genetic difference between a White female and a Black female is 6% of 20% of 1%. It's tiny. Yet when Dolezal tried to claim she was "trans-Black," the Black culture almost universally rejected her. They said that she not only was genetically not Black, but they also appealed to culture and said that Dolezal could not relate to the cultural experience of living as a Black person in a White culture. All this is true and understandable. But let's look at who else Dolezal is. She is a female with absolutely no Y chromosome in her twenty-three chromosome pairs. There is a much bigger difference between a man and a woman than between a White woman and a Black woman. But if Rachel Dolezal showed up at your workplace and if she checked the box that said she was a Black woman, she could be accused of lying and face the consequences. But if Rachel Dolezal showed up at your workplace and claimed to be a man, you could be forced to address her as "he," allow her to use the men's bathroom and any other accommodation she asked for.

We have now reached a point (2021) where feminized leaders of US corporations engage in rounds of virtue signaling in an effort to appease the "woke mob" and be in the inner circle of their corporate

---

[52] Corporate Equality Index-2021, www.hrc.org/resources/corporate-equality-index.

associates. Due to the feminization of our culture, an organization's performance, no matter how important its mission, is now secondary to its ability to provide a "space" for cozy group therapy.

Social Justice in Politics

The real story here is that Social Justice is not something that has necessarily been on the campaign platform of many elected officials, but it has been able to take the "long march through institutions" as described by the Cultural Marxists. The same people who used to say "you can't legislate morality" are busy trying to legislate their morality of Social Justice through the Equality Act. With the election of Joe Biden, there will be more efforts to use the federal government to punish those who don't go along with the new religion of Social Justice. Federal government agencies, instead of cutting their budgets and freeing more resources for real assistance to poor people, are engaged in the same virtue signaling and CRT training that is happening in large corporations and other institutions.

Label Jail and Canceling

One of the other weapons used to passively move people around on the Personal Identity Matrix is name-calling or labeling. Our culture plays right into this because name-calling or labeling is often a lazy way to make a judgment about someone. If you disagree with anybody trying to move men into this area or disagree with anyone trying to motivate women to be less godly and more masculine, you will be called any number of names: misogynist, feminist hater, homophobe, hatemonger, etc.—Another weapon used by feminists against men is the concept of victimhood. The idea is that all men owe all women something because men as a collective have victimized women. That used to be called guilt by association and was accepted as philosophically wrong, but that has changed. People who advocate the idea that "binary is bad" tend to label people more than any other group. This is hypocritical because most of the labels they use force a binary condition. Either you are, or are not, the pejorative they are calling you. The Social Justice crowd tries to make the rules and "funnel" anyone who does not think like them into "label jail." A good example of the "funnel" is the bumper sticker that says, "Stop pretending your racism is patriotism." In other words, if you support your country, you are a racist.

Labels can be useful to facilitate communication but only if they are true. Common tactics of egalitarians, Marxists, and others who are fighting against the Christian worldview are as follows:

1) Use a media campaign to create and demonize a label.
2) Either lie about someone or use a "broad brush" to link someone to a demonized category.
3) Put that person in "label jail."
4) Advocate punishment for all people who have that label.
5) Hold out no hope of forgiveness unless the person "repents" and becomes an "ally."
6) Politically marginalize the beliefs and views of everyone who is in "label jail."
7) Punish (current punishment is "canceling") everyone who has been placed in "label jail."

Here is a chart of common label jails:

Pejorative (Label Jail)	Used On	Endgame
Racist	Anyone who opposes redistribution of wealth and power from the "haves" to the "have-nots". It is only primarily applied in the United States with the assumption that Blacks are universally oppressed by Whites. This is textbook Marxism.	Marxism
Misogynist	Anyone who believes men and women are different.	Egalitarianism
Patriarchal	Anyone who does not fully support feminism.	Feminism
Bigot	Can be used for anyone who tries to defend Biblical boundaries.	Egalitarianism
Homophobe	Anyone who refuses to be an ally.	To Criminalize Christianity
Xenophobe	Anyone who defends national borders.	Ostensibly Open Borders and Globalism, but it is primarily applied to Western nations.
Nationalist	Anyone who supports their country instead of wanting to submit it to any other (usually globalist) authority.	Globalism
Extremist	Anyone who believes in objective truth that disagrees with the "labeler".	Usually either Egalitarianism or Marxism, used in propaganda relating to smaller issues.
White Supremacist	Applied to Conservatives and Christians.	Usually Marxism, eventually Global Egalitarian Marxism
Anti-Science	Anyone who does not believe politically correct "science".	Originally only Evolution, but lately "science" has been weaponized pragmatically.
Conspiracy Theorist	Anyone who does not follow the MSM (mainstream media) story line.	Global Egalitarian Marxism
Sexist	Anyone who believes men and women are different.	Feminism
Islamophobe	Anyone who believes that Islam is anything but a universally peaceful religion where all adherents are incapable of any evil thoughts, words, or actions.	Global Egalitarian Marxism
Transphobe	Anyone who believes the Biblical standards of sexuality.	Egalitarianism
Christian Nationalist	Anyone who is either a Christian or has an level of allegiance to their country.	Global Egalitarian Marxism

Table 25. Label jails.

As usual, the people who use these "cancel culture" tactics are not randomly trying to improve the morality of the planet but are working to accomplish something. They are certainly trying to destroy the existing order and build something new. In their minds, they are building the "New World Order." The endgame is to put all Christians and God Himself in label jail. Wherever possible, those attempting to build the "New World Order" will punish Christians. But the "New World Order" will ultimately be destroyed by God, and those who participate in it will be punished by God.

Weaponizing History

When Amy Coney Barrett was nominated by Donald Trump for Supreme Court Justice, everyone expected her to be attacked by Socialists/Marxists.

Ibram X. Kendi went straight to the fable projection playbook with this tweet, "Some White colonizers 'adopted' Black children. They 'civilized' these 'savage' children in the 'superior' ways of White people, using them as props in their lifelong pictures of denial, while cutting the biological parents of these children out of the picture of humanity."[53]

This is a great example from the CRT playbook for how to weaponize history to destroy something in the present. Here is their formula:

1) Make up a non-verifiable story about the past.
2) Fabricate a moral judgment into the story.
3) Color code the story to facilitate transferring the moral judgment through space and time to someone else.
4) Use the moral judgment to destroy an existing person, law, or institution.

Many people understandably reacted by accusing Kendi of being a hateful racist. This may be true, but he is actually up to

---

[53] Ibram X. Kendi, Twitter, September 26, 2020.

something more sinister. It's hard to believe, but there is evidence that Kendi may only be pretending to be a racist. Kendi has received $10 million in donations from the White male CEO of Twitter, Jack Dorsey. Here is something to look for in the messaging from people like Kendi. You will often see the word "white" coupled with the word "always." That's because these race-baiters have a deeper motive to convince people that western civilization is not redeemable in its current form. They think that "whiteness" is the evil spirit that has possessed capitalism and Christianity, and if capitalism and Christianity are destroyed, "whiteness" will magically disappear. The endgame for Dorsey and Kendi is to paint the lower right corner of the political matrix as evil, which will enable the desired move to the upper left:

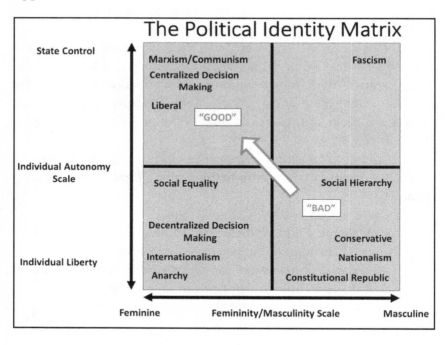

There are other examples of using weaponizing history against the lower right quadrant. Here are examples of some other ridiculous ideas that have been promoted:

1) The oppressive early colonists of the United States were more interested in using guns against slaves than against British soldiers, so they created the second amendment.
2) The second amendment is inherently racist and must be destroyed.

Here is another variation:

1) Christianity was used by the oppressive early colonists to control slaves.
2) The first amendment is inherently racist and must be destroyed.

Selectively obsessing on past oppressions has become a full-time job for many left-wing professors. Their endgame is the assertion that the United States is irreparably tainted by "whiteness" and, therefore, must be destroyed.

A New ~~Coalition~~ Hierarchy of Victims

For all the energy around buzzwords like equality, equity, diversity, inclusion, etc., destroyed hierarchies are always replaced by other hierarchies. Even communist countries have a hierarchy between communist party members and nonparty members. Of course, the communist dictator is the oppressor, and everyone else is oppressed.

According to a recent article in the WSJ, transgenderism is now a threat to homosexuality. "Lesbians have been denounced as "bigots" for expressing a reluctance to date men who identify as women. The successful normalization of homosexuality could be undermined by miring it in an untenable ideology."[54]

A recent episode on HGTV featured a "throuple," a polyamorous threesome composed of a man and two women.[55] What's next, "throuple divorce?" What if two people in the throuple want to be divorced from the third. Do two pay alimony to one? How will the courts sort it all out? The inevitable result is chaos, and it's even harder to achieve any semblance of "equality" in the midst of such chaos.

Inevitably the promises of egalitarianism will under-deliver. Once you program a culture to feel cheated by "micro-aggressions," there is little chance anyone will ever be happy, no matter what organizational structures you modify, destroy, or create.

Identity-Based Religions

There are growing religions that continue the thesis that your physical DNA is more important than your "spiritual DNA" and, just like CRT, make a religion out of it. The "oppression porn" seen in Cultural Marxism then becomes theology to these new religions because historical oppression is used as "proof" that the adherents to these religions are the "chosen people." These are the primary religions that people with identity issues are susceptible to:

1) Black Hebrew Israelites
2) Hebrew-Nation Building
3) Nation of Islam
4) Aryan Nations

---

[54] Neil Munro, "WSJ: Elites Enthusiasm for Transgenderism Endangers Gay, Lesbian Youth," February 15, 2020, https://www.breitbart.com/politics/2020/02/15/wsj-elites-enthusiasm-for-transgenderism-endangers-gay-lesbian-youth/.

[55] Michael Brown, "HGTV and 'Throuple:' Mindlessly Careening Our Way Down the Slippery Slope," February 18, 2020, https://www.christianpost.com/voices/hgtv-and-throuple-mindlessly-careening-our-way-down-the-slippery-slope.html.

Here is a summary of the beliefs[56], [57] of these groups:

Belief	Black Hebrew Israelites*	Hebrew Nation Building*	Nation of Islam**	Aryan Nations
Believe they are a "chosen people" based on bloodline.	•	•	•	•
Believe that the Jews of the Bible are actually African-American slaves.	•	•		
Believe that the Jews of the Bible are actually European white people.				•
Believe Africans are sub-human.				•
Believe Jews are descendants of the devil.				•
Most believe in a Jewish Messiah called Yahshuah Ben Yah (Jesus son of God) but are skeptical that this is the same "Jesus of Nazareth" worshipped by Christians. They often believe in "calling upon Yahshuah Ben Yah".	•	•		
Deny the Trinitarian nature of God.	•			
Deny the divinity of Yahshuah Ben Yah.	•			
Deny the doctrine of hell.	•			
Deny Justification by Faith.	•			
Deny Penal Substitution.	•			
Generally see some ethic groups as incapable of being saved.	•	•		
Believe the white race was formed by selective breeding 6,000 years ago by a black scientist named Yakub.			•	
Believe that Semitic Jews seek to control the world through banking.			•	•
Believe that Hamitic "Fake" Jews seek to control the world through banking.	•	•		
Advocates destroying the United States.	tacitly	tacitly	•	
Advocates a separate state for black Americans.			•	
Believes in Allah as god and Muhammed as prophet.			•	
Number of followers.			50,000	
Evangelizes in prisons.			•	
Advocates following Biblical Law.	•	•		
Segregationist by race.	•			

* beliefs are not homogeneous among groups
**https://www.ibtimes.com/what-nation-islam-history-beliefs-practices-religious-movement-1829370

Table 26. Identity-based religions.

---

[56] "The Black Hebrew Israelite Cult, Exposed!" https://descendantsofnoahh.wordpress.com/2015/04/26/the-black-hebrew-israelite-cult-exposed/.

[57] "Four Important Things to Know about the Black Hebrew Israelites," https://pulpitandpen.org/2019/12/13/four-important-things-to-know-about-the-black-hebrew-isr.

These identity-based religions share some commonalities. One is Gnosticism. They claim to know new or special ways of interpreting the Bible and history. Like a lot of Gnostics, they seem hesitant to document exactly what they believe.

The largest of these groups is the Nation of Islam. The Nation of Islam (NOI) simultaneously advocates the establishment of a separate state for Black Americans while wanting to destroy the United States. NOI is considered by orthodox Islam to be a nonaffiliated cult.

It is difficult to determine the size of the other groups. One sect that has been growing lately is the Black Hebrew Israelites (BHI). If you go downtown and see a street gang that looks like they are wearing costumes from the movie *Ben Hur*, those are the Black Hebrew Israelites. The core belief of BHI is that Black Americans are the true Israelites of the Bible, and everyone who is typically considered a Jew is actually a "fake Jew" who descended from Ham. I have read and seen some bizarre beliefs from people in these BHI groups. Some believe that White people came from some sort of "leprosy mutants" of Black people. One BHI leader has advocated killing 200 million White people as a sacrifice for the sins of Black people. He evidently thinks White people are perfect since that is the condition given for sacrifices in the Old Testament. There are several factions (or "camps") of Black Hebrew Israelites in the United States. Many men in these camps advocate following Old Testament law, but they swear like sailors. Just like the "Aryan Nation" religion, the Black Hebrew Israelites believe that they are a superior race to the other races. The three groups (BHI, HNB, and Aryan Nations) that claim to follow the Bible have a big problem with their belief that "we are God's chosen people" because the Bible is so well connected to both history and geography.

The Hebrew Nation Building (HNB) group has similar beliefs to the BHI but is more accepting of the New Testament and evidently believes in the resurrection of Jesus, although they will insist on calling Him "Yeshua" and also insist that He is Black. However, many of the HNB have a somewhat veiled hatred of White people.

You can see all three groups (BHI, HNB, and NOI) defending each other on "Black supremacy twitter" even though their alleged spiritual beliefs should make them enemies. But physical DNA is more important than spiritual beliefs to these identity religions, so that is not surprising.

The Aryan Nations groups are a mirror image of the Black Hebrew Israelites. If you take either group and substitute the word "white" for "black," and vice versa, the theology is remarkably similar. This is ironic since both groups hate each other. I am not sure which belief system was developed first, but one evidently copied the other at some point.

All these identity-based religions are contrary to Scripture on varying points. Here is what Paul says to Timothy in I Timothy 1:3–4:

> As I urged you upon my departure for Macedonia, remain on at Ephesus so that you may instruct certain men not to teach strange doctrines, nor to pay attention to myths and endless genealogies, which give rise to mere speculation rather than furthering the administration of God which is by faith.

If African Americans are God's "chosen people" (meaning descendants of Abraham), there are many passages in the Bible that directly challenge that belief. One is that Moses's wife was Black. This is a huge issue because, according to the Bible, Moses, Aaron, and Miriam were descendants of Abraham. Here is Numbers 12:1–2:

> Then Miriam and Aaron spoke against Moses because of the Cushite woman whom he had married (for he had married a Cushite woman); and they said, "Has the Lord indeed spoken only through Moses? Has He not spoken through us as well?" And the Lord heard it.

Cushites were descendants of Ham, and here Moses's wife is clearly described as being Black. It challenges truth and logic to assert that all four people in the passage (Moses, Moses's wife, Aaron, and Miriam) were Black.

Pastor David Lynn has a good rebuttal to the assertion of any race being superior:

1) All people are made in the image of God.
2) All people came from Adam and Eve.
3) If the original man was Black, Cain brought murder into the world.
4) Martin Luther King spoke about judging people by the content of their character.
5) What about albino Blacks?

I would add that any notion of superiority is often situation and location-dependent. If your car is stuck, you probably want the biggest, strongest men you can find to push the car out. However, if your car is broken, those same men might have hands that are too big to fit in the engine compartment to repair your car, so you might want your mechanic to be smaller. Which men are superior? It depends on the situation you are in.

What is the endgame of these religions? They don't usually say, but occasionally, they will talk about building a nation, which probably gives away what they really want, although maybe they mainly want to help divide and conquer the United States.

The BHI, HNB, and NOI are united in their opinion that Black people should be paid "reparations" because of historical slavery and discrimination. Here are some very real issues with the concept of "reparations:"

1) Reparations won't work unless structural issues are addressed, such as family structure.
2) Reparations are taken from a government that is running a deficit. This means that reparations will simply steal from future generations of Black children.

3) Slaves were paid with food, clothing, and shelter. This complicates the math for determining the dollar amount of reparations.
4) Descendants of slaves have already received government assistance in one form or another.
5) Over 365,000 White men died fighting for the Union Army in the Civil War to end slavery. Would the descendants of freed slaves owe the descendants of these soldiers reparations?

The net impact of these identity-based religions (or cults) is two-fold. First, they are leading people astray spiritually. Secondly, their race obsession is working hand in glove with the Cultural Marxists to destroy the West in general and the United States in particular. Imagine if you asked a group of White Christians, "Would you rather hang out with Black Christians or White Satan worshipers?" or if you asked Black Christians, "Who do you trust more, White Christians or Black Satan worshipers?" People in identity-based religions genuinely struggle with questions like that. The Christian conversion process was described by Jesus as being "born again." This describes a spiritual transformation that transcends the physical.

Zionism (or what I call hyper-Zionism) is also worth mentioning. While it probably makes political sense for the civil government of the United States to support Israel, this does not automatically mean that churches should blindly support Israel and all Jews simply because they are "God's chosen people." The Great Commission applies the same to Israel and the Jews as it does to any other nation or people. When you evaluate both the Old and New Testaments, it is clear that while the Jews were established as a chosen nation, there were laws in the Old Testament that allowed people who were not descendants of Abraham, Isaac, or Jacob to be a part of the Hebrew nation. That is why there were some people in the lineage of Christ who were not Hebrews. As a citizen of the United States, it makes sense to consider the nation of Israel a political ally. But as a

Christian, we have to be careful about automatically assuming Jews are spiritual allies.

A powerful example of the "spiritual DNA" that I am talking about is in Matthew 8:5–13.

> And when Jesus entered Capernaum, a centurion came to Him, imploring Him, and saying, "Lord, my servant is lying paralyzed at home, fearfully tormented." Jesus said to him, "I will come and heal him." But the centurion said, "Lord, I am not worthy for You to come under my roof, but just say the word, and my servant will be healed. For I also am a man under authority, with soldiers under me; and I say to this one, 'Go!' and he goes, and to another, 'Come!' and he comes, and to my slave, 'Do this!' and he does it." Now when Jesus heard this, He marveled and said to those who were following, "Truly I say to you, I have not found such great faith with anyone in Israel. I say to you that many will come from east and west, and recline at the table with Abraham, Isaac and Jacob in the kingdom of heaven; but the sons of the kingdom will be cast out into the outer darkness; in that place there will be weeping and gnashing of teeth." And Jesus said to the centurion, "Go; it shall be done for you as you have believed." And the servant was healed that very moment.

The centurion was Roman, a Gentile. His faith was said to be greater than anyone in Israel. So what was on the inside was more important than skin color or bloodline.

CHAPTER 11

Using the Personal Identity Matrix to Transform Yourself and Your Family

This book has analyzed much of what has gone wrong in our culture. It is intimidating to think of pushing back against the forces that are arrayed against us. But since there are theoretically infinite ways to mess something up and there are far fewer ways to do things correctly, the solutions I propose are not easy, but they are far less complicated than the problems we are seeing.

The most important force multiplier I have identified is that if men and women (especially the men) will start to move in the proper direction on the Personal Identity Matrix, then it will enable other good things to start happening. For example, if young men and women are in the right places on the chart, they are increasing the odds of being a good spouse. Opposites attract, and well-behaved men and women don't always make history, but they do tend to stay married.

Restoring Masculinity in Christian Men

Remember the story from chapter 1? Here it is again:

> Imagine a church staff meeting at the First Church of Anytown, USA. It's probably a Monday or Tuesday morning. The pastor, assistant pastor, and

all the church leadership are there discussing the typical things they would be discussing every week—things such as hospital visits, funerals, various maintenance items, and the next special events of the church. These are all good things. There is nothing wrong with anything they are talking about. But suddenly, the people in the meeting notice that the pastor has a laser dot on his forehead. Then another laser dot appears on his forehead. Then all the other people in the staff notice that everyone in the meeting has two laser dots on their foreheads. There are two snipers aiming at each person in the meeting. Immediately, the conversation completely changes. This church is also in a crossfire. Each of you is also a crossfire, and you probably don't even know it.

The point of the story is that not only is your Christianity, but also your masculinity (if you are male) is under attack. It would be unfair if I exhorted men to simply "Man up!" (I dislike the phrase anyway. If you have played pickup basketball, you know that "Man up!" simply means pick out who on the other team you are guarding.) But anyway, saying "Man up!" without explaining that your culture is actively and systemically fighting male masculinity would only lead to frustration. So developing your and/or your son's masculinity is going to be tougher than it used to be. You can expect serious resistance at times.

When something big goes wrong, there are usually multiple variables that get out of control. The good news is that by working on one additional variable, it can have a force multiplier effect and restore order from chaos. Hopefully, I have shown the importance of families and churches developing masculine men and feminine women. The process of developing masculine men and feminine women should be a core objective of families and churches and not looked upon as a parallel "nice-to-have."

Fathers should take ownership of modeling Christian masculinity to their sons.

A great way to rebuild your spiritual foundation to understand who you are as a man is to do an in-depth study of Genesis. There is a powerful Genesis commentary called "The Genesis Record" written by Henry Morris that is a great place to start.

Another great book for men to study is *Masculine Christianity* by Zachary M. Garris.

Restoring Femininity in Christian Women

Due to the strong and constant messaging that the feminists are broadcasting to women, Christian women are going to have to unlearn a lot of lies that they have been told. But first, there is a trust issue that has to be addressed. Because feminists have done a good job of playing the "identity card," many Christian women will trust feminists before they trust God or God's Word, the Bible. But can you really trust someone who claims to be for equality (and "equity") when they advocate aborting children?

Step one is to understand and admit that feminism has hurt women. Women need to be told that there are things in life that are more fulfilling than what is held out to them as the "holy grail" (life in a cubicle).

The next foundational step is to understand that feminists advertise selfishness, but it is not as fulfilling as advertised. Selfishness has proven to be overrated, especially from a mental health standpoint. All women should have the right not to be feminists if they don't want to be.

The final challenge is to understand that if you are a Christian woman, especially a young one, you owe it to yourself to do a deep study of God's design for women. Too many pastors are de facto feminists, so you probably have not been taught this, even in church. As mentioned earlier, I highly recommend the book *Eve in Exile* by Rebekah Merkle.[58]

---

[58] Rebekah Merkle, *Eve in Exile and the Restoration of Femininity* (Moscow, Idaho: Canonpress, 2016).

CHAPTER 12

Using the Personal Identity Matrix to Transform the Church

In the book of Acts, the early church is dedicated to changing people. Too often, the modern church is functioning as a weather vane and is attempting to flow with the culture. It is crucial that the church fulfill its God-ordained mission. Many churches have become so feminized that they will not admit there is a universal problem that is destroying all of them. Here is my best summary of the problem: churches are no longer able to function correctly because of the breakdown of the family. The family is being destroyed because of the breakdown in the institution of marriage. Marriage is being destroyed because of feminism. Rollo Tomassi says in *The Rational Male: Religion*,[59] "Ask any tribe of the manosphere, and they'll probably have a detailed explanation as to why marriage today is the single worst decision a man can make in his life." Meanwhile, pastors continue to blindly marry couples without acknowledging that statistically, they are setting their men up for destruction. So it is foundational that the church starts making disciples again. Disciples make good spouses.

---

[59] Rollo Tomassi, *The Rational Male: Religion* (Reno, Nevada: Counterflow Media, 2020).

Does Your Pastor Need a Performance Review?

I don't mean to be disrespecting pastors as a group. That would be unfair. There are a lot of amazing, gutsy pastors out there. But there are too many cowards and "wolves in sheep's clothing" currently in the ministry. Figure out where your pastor is on the Personal Identity Matrix, then decide where your pastor is trending. If your pastor is not trending toward masculine Christianity, you and some other men in leadership need to challenge him to do so. If your pastor is still not trending toward developing himself as a masculine image-bearer, you need to start looking for another church.

Fixing Marriage

Let's look at the Personal Identity Matrix and see how marriage fits into it.

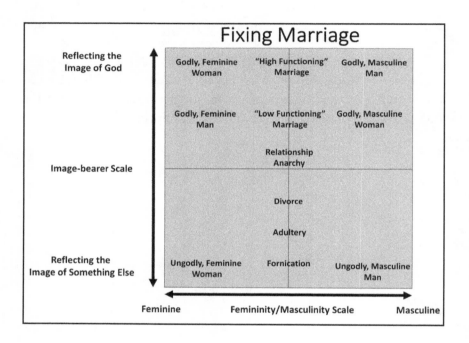

The chart above shows various combinations of husband and wife on the Personal Identity Matrix. The chart assumes that the husband and wife are spiritually in the same place but "unequally yoked" marriages (Godly, feminine woman married to an ungodly, masculine man, for example) obviously occur as well. The type of marriage is described in the middle column of the chart.

Marriage has degenerated into a sloppy semiformal contract. For all the theological talk about covenants, pastors tend to put a lot of effort into flowery verbal vows that would be far more useful if they were cleaned up and put on paper. "Covenant marriages" (legally called a prenuptial agreement) should be contracts that are facilitated by the church. Specific penalties for adultery and abandonment should be written in. These penalties should address the potential loss of custody and impacts to both alimony and child support in the event of bad behavior. If you think this is extreme, have you ever bought a house, even a small house? Compare that house purchase contract with the typical marriage vows you hear at a wedding. Think about which "transaction" is more important. When was the last time you had a young man and a young woman get married in your church? It is sad that it does not happen as often anymore, but your church should work toward developing the right kind of potential spouses and then work to make weddings happen for those people. Most modern pastors assume that their church is filled with fornication. This makes them want to rush couples down the aisle like it's a spiritual carwash. Any pastor performing a wedding needs to take that wedding very seriously.

Restoring Christianity in the Church

Pastors are human. They also feel like it is their Christian duty to respond to the concerns of their congregation. But the core mission of a church is not to "love everybody" or "meet the needs of people," although there is a biblical basis for both of those. The core mission of that church is to defend the theology of that particular church. A major issue is that most churches have the wrong concerns, so the pastors are responding to issues that probably should not be high-priority issues. If you're a man, once you have committed to being in the right place on the Personal Identity Matrix, find some other men in your church who share your interest. Then you can put together a core group of men who have the proper concerns for the spiritual life of your church. Then you need to meet with your pastor and see how committed he is to ministering to the men and their needs. You may not be in the right church.

Your church leadership must have the courage to preach and study an entire book of the Bible instead of cherry-picked topical studies. The book of Nehemiah is a good place to start for recalibrating the mission of a church or group of believers. Another great way to reset your church's priorities is to do a Sunday school or sermon series on the book of Acts. The early church was very masculine as an organization and played offense instead of defense. The book of Acts is not about redecorating or organizing support groups. But there is something both beautiful and therapeutic about staying on your mission.

Beyond your local congregation, your church should forge relationships with other churches in order to be united against the current and looming attacks on the church at large.

Restoring Correct Masculinity and Femininity in the Church

There is some simple direction from Scripture about how to restore the correct masculinity and femininity in your church. It's in Titus 2:2–8.

> Older men are to be temperate, dignified, sensible, sound in faith, in love, in perseverance. Older women likewise are to be reverent in their behavior, not malicious gossips nor enslaved to much wine, teaching what is good, so that they may encourage the young women to love their husbands, to love their children, to be sensible, pure, workers at home, kind, being subject to their own husbands, so that the word of God will not be dishonored. Likewise urge the young men to be sensible; in all things show yourself to be an example of good deeds, with purity in doctrine, dignified, sound in speech which is beyond reproach, so that the opponent will be put to shame, having nothing bad to say about us.

The bottom line here is that most churches have buckled under egalitarian pressure to make everything "coed." This is not biblical. Older men should be teaching younger men, and older women should be teaching younger women. This one change will correctly model godly masculinity and femininity for the younger people.

Call Out and Cast Out the Trojan Horses

There is a balance with this one. People need to be warned about false prophets and wolves in sheep's clothing, but you don't want to give these evil people free publicity. Many Trojan horses have an online following, and that's how they do most of their damage. Do not be afraid to warn people within your circle of influence of these false teachers.

> For many deceivers have gone out into the world, those who do not acknowledge Jesus Christ as coming in the flesh. This is the deceiver and the antichrist. Watch yourselves, that you do not lose what we have accomplished, but that you may receive a full reward. Anyone who goes too far and does not abide in the teaching of Christ, does not have God; the one who abides in the teaching, he has both the Father and the Son. If anyone comes to you and does not bring this teaching, do not receive him into your house, and do not give him a greeting; for the one who gives him a greeting participates in his evil deeds. (II John 7–11)

At the local level, make the hijackers build their own organization instead of taking over your organization. We simply don't consider how much effort these hijacking Trojan horses put into taking over an organization when all along, they have had the freedom to build their own. Excommunication and church discipline were standard practices in years past, but not now. So many churches have been spiritually neutralized by Trojan horses.

Find the Moral Compass

Do not hand your moral compass over to someone who has none. We have reached a point where the worst behaved, foul-mouthed, hateful people have become the experts on morality. The modern church is so legalism-phobic that it cannot or will not make a moral judgment on almost anything. We are now allowing non-Christians to tell us how to be better Christians. Meanwhile, the message inside most churches continues to give people permission to sin. If you pay attention, you will notice that most people have out-sourced their consciences to the media. If their favorite media outlet is upset, they will be upset.

Stop Saying These Things

In an effort to tell people what they want to hear, you can hear messaging in many churches that is dangerous at the least. Here are some statements that pastors and church leaders need to stop saying:

1) "Don't judge!" Yes, this one opens a theological can of worms, but behavior always matters. Watch how and when you hear "Don't judge!" If you find it being selectively applied, that's a big problem.
2) "God's love is unconditional." There is a heaven and a hell. Without repentance and faith in Christ, one will not get into heaven. To tell people that God's love is unconditional is sloppy and dangerous. See Ligonier Ministries "Is God's Love Unconditional?" for a deeper analysis of this import-ant issue.[60]
3) "God has already forgiven you for every sin you are going to commit in your life." Theological issues aside, do you really want your teenager to hear this one?
4) "We must avoid us versus them." This statement is a vari-ation of the feminized "Thou shalt not fight back." The

---

[60] https://www.ligonier.org/blog/unconditional-love-god/.

word "them" occurs 6,429 times in the Bible. The word "us" occurs in the Bible 1,449 times. This statement also comes from the naive assumption that there are two types of religious identities in the world—those who have heard the gospel and accepted Christ and those who have not. The Bible prophesies an increase in the end-times of a third category that, due to cowardly wishful thinking, many Christians do not want to admit exists—those who have heard the Gospel, rejected it, and now hate God and all who are associated with Him.

5) "Love yourself!" Don't worry, everybody already does. If someone says, "I am so ugly. I hate myself," it doesn't really make sense. If you really hated yourself, you would be glad you were ugly. A better statement is "Love what God has given you."

6) "All are welcome here." It sounds "nice," but anybody who says it is lying, whether they know it or not. It's usually virtue signaling for the LGBTQ community. Try showing up in a MAGA hat.

7) "We need to just focus on _____." This is yet another lazy and cowardly excuse to cherry-pick the Bible. The alleged motive may be peacemaking, but it will end up being appeasement.

Start Saying These Things

One of the few positives that have come from the COVID-19 pandemic is that a forgotten word is making a comeback in churches. That word is "repent." Signs that say to repent can now be seen in various places, and that did not happen for years. This is a good message that we all need to hear.

If you decide to proclaim the truth, there is one big advantage you have. There can be infinite lies about an issue, but there is only one true account of that issue. In this book, I have addressed many lies and errors that our culture is brainwashing people with. You don't have to try to debate against every lie to proclaim the truth.

One of the main lessons we learn from studying the book of Acts is that your message is more important than you are. Instead of cherry-picked self-help messages, there needs to be a reemphasis on The Great Commission. We should be thinking of "the whole Word for the whole world."

Many pastors and churches are evidently so terrified of losing their 501.c.3 status that they refuse to speak to any civil issues. For example, no pastor or church (that I am aware of) has spoken out against the discrimination of the church insurance situation. Maybe if a small few spoke up, it would encourage others.

In the early stages of the "culture war," it was common to see bumper stickers that said, "Question Authority." Okay, then it should be fair game to question those who question authority. We should be questioning the following:

1) The theory of evolution
2) Critical Race Theory
3) Everyone's basis for right and wrong
4) Abortion (Where is the "equity" in this issue?)

There are many other issues in our culture that Christians would be talking about, at least in their church, if we can add some masculinity back into our leaders.

Initiation Rites: Making Men Out of Boys

One of the traits of masculinity we explored in an earlier chapter is the existence of a "rite of passage" that many cultures have used in order to signify the passage of a boy into manhood. I felt that I needed to include a sample rite because our culture is currently doing a terrible job of turning boys into masculine men. This section may come off to you as a little "over the top," but this information will hopefully stimulate more thought of how you may want to implement a similar rite. You may want to try to accomplish the same objectives in the rite below informally and over time.

From *The Church Impotent* by Leon Podles:[61]

> Gordon Dalbey, a United Church of Christ minister, observed Nigerian rituals in which boys are taken from the world of women and inducted into the world of men and the sacred realities of their tribe. He has formulated a Christian puberty ritual for boys to counteract the lack of male participation in the Church.
>
> His suggestion for the ritual is this: The father, pretending to go somewhere else [not sure I like the deception here, but feel free to modify], goes to the church to prepare to induct his son into manhood. With the pastor and other men, he arrives unannounced back at his house. His mother (uninformed about the event, which is for men only) is hesitant, but as the men outside sing "Rise Up O Men of God," the boy breaks from his mother and joins his father and the men of the church. As he joins them, the men sing "A Mighty Fortress." The men and boys then go to a campground for discipline and instruction, which would include:
>
> - An opening worship in which each boy is taught to memorize Romans 12:1–2, offering himself to God's service and opening himself to let God transform him inwardly during the initiation period
> - Time to remember the men from whom the boy comes: stories of his father and grandfather and American history

---

[61] Leon Podles, *The Church Impotent: The Feminization of Christianity* (Dallas, Texas: Spence Publishing Company, 1999).

- Time to remember the God from whom all men come: Bible stories and biblical standards of behavior
- Learning to pray, both alone and with others
- A time of fasting during which the boy is taught its biblical purpose
- Teaching the nature of sexuality and how to relate to women with compassion and strength
- Aptitude testing for professional skills, followed by a general session in which the men sit as a panel and share frankly their jobs, inviting questions afterward
- Rigorous physical exercise
- Daily individual prayer, Bible reading, and journal keeping
- Prayer and counseling for each boy to heal inner emotional wounds
- Talks by much older, godly men about what life was like when they were boys and what their faith has meant to them
- A closing worship service in which the men call each boy forward, lay hands on him, and pray for him to receive the Holy Spirit as in the traditional rite of confirmation.[62]

At the very least, this should get you thinking about the importance of letting boys know that they are expected to turn into men.

Reevaluating Community in the Church

In their book, *You Will be Made to Care*, Erick Erickson and Bill Blankschaen interview Ravi Zacharias about community. Although his behavior is now suspect, to say the least, Zacharias's ability to

---

[62] Ibid.

analyze complex issues is still hard to dispute. Ravi explains, "For the Christian worldview, there are three starting points: identity—who we are. If you go back to the laws of logic, the first law of logic is a law of identity. If A, then not non-A, and then there is intimacy, how do we find the purity of one intimate relationship, which we all long for? The third is the outworking of the community. We all seek identity, intimacy, and community. From the Christian point of view, that community moves in the direction of worship. Yes, it's not a perfect community. Yes, we have fallibilities, and we have weaknesses. Sometimes, hypocrisies are revealed, but just because we have our failings in our shortcomings does not mean we should remove the direction in which we want to walk. And that is the whole point of the New Testament, a community of worship. The book of Acts is really what happened when believers had that belief in common. You have to have certain shared identities, certain shared meanings of the past. Cultural revolutions become realities when those shared meanings of the past are lost. Community is vital." [63]

As the persecution of Christians becomes more and more socially acceptable, the protection that a community of believers can offer becomes more and more important.

Reengineer Seminaries and Christian Colleges

What do Harvard, Yale, and Princeton have in common, other than being in the Ivy League and being bastions of anti-biblical thought? Each of them was founded as an orthodox Christian college. Seminaries and Bible colleges have proven to be failed models. They are centralized and subsidized, and this makes them vulnerable to trying to impress the world instead of changing it.

---

[63] Erick Erickson and Bill Blankschaen, *You Will be Made to Care* (Washington, DC: Regnery Publishing, 2016).

The chart below breaks down the problem with Christian schools and seminaries:

	Teach good information	Model good behavior	Opportunity to apply new knowledge	Teach bad information	Model bad behavior
Traditional Family	X	X	X		
Biblical Church	X	X	X		
Christian School	X				
Seminary	X				
Public School				X	X
Public College				X	X

Table 27. Educational process of major institutions.

In this chart, we are looking at historical institutions of education: the traditional family, Biblical churches, Christian schools, seminaries, public schools, and public colleges. These institutions are compared on the metrics of teaching good information, modeling good behavior, and the opportunity to apply what the students have learned. You can see the inherent advantages of the teaching and training from a traditional family and a biblical church. Both give children an opportunity to learn good information, see good behavior modeled, and find out if what they have been taught actually works. Seminaries are designed to disseminate good information, and that's it. If bad information starts being taught, then a seminary becomes a culturally destructive force, like public schools and colleges. It can also drag down an entire denomination. Christian colleges and seminaries also fall victim to trying to be like the large public universities that are spending millions of dollars on research to come up with new discoveries. When an institution is doing research, the goal is to find new information. So what's new is inherently more valuable than what's true. The seminaries don't have the million-dollar research budget, so they tend to start presenting false religions like Critical Race Theory as if they have discovered something new and fascinating.

The early church did not establish any seminaries or Bible colleges. If churches would apply biblical standards to leadership and stop counting degrees, it would decrease the demand for seminaries and Bible colleges, and that would be a good thing.

CHAPTER 13

Using the Political Identity Matrix to Transform the Culture

The Political Identity Matrix is useful in understanding a given political situation, but always remember that the Personal Identity Matrix is foundational to having the self-governed people that make a culture thrive. You saw the chart below in a previous chapter:

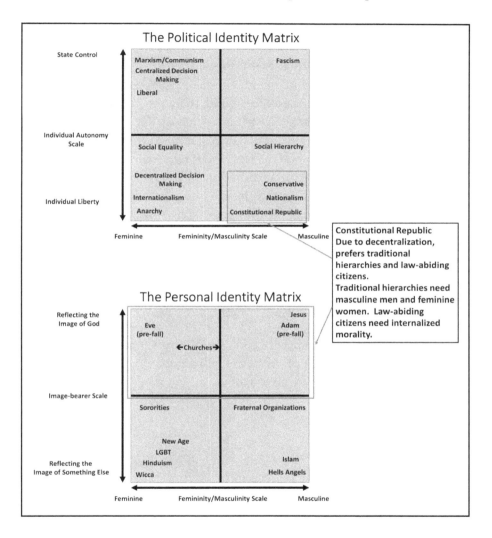

It is of vital importance that we follow biblical mandates to create "image-bearers" for Christ. The men must be masculine, and the women must be feminine. All must be self-controlled image-bearers.

The Post-Truth Era

In a feminized culture, "truth" is determined by feelings, majority rule, bullies, a mob, or "experts," whose expertise is often determined by an oligarchy of platforms.

In our modern culture, many times, the truth of a statement is evaluated by its therapeutic value. People have become more interested in lies that make them feel good than the truth that might make them want to change. Truth is not cheap. Truth is becoming scarce, and you are going to have to work hard to find it.

In George Orwell's book, *1984*, the totalitarian government has a Ministry of Truth. The main function of the Ministry of Truth is to destroy all truth and replace it with lies. In her blog on americanthinker.com,[64] Andrea Widburg explains how "woke scholars" are now claiming that two plus two does not always equal four and that two plus two can sometimes equal five. Instead of searching for truth, these "woke scholars" are trying to do the following:

1) Attack the meaning of ideas via deconstruction to dissolve them.
2) Promote the idea that racism/White supremacy is baked into every area of Western civilization.
3) Minimize the value of truth.

---

[64] Andrea Widburg, "Leftists Go after Two Plus Two Equals Four," August 5, 2020, https://www.americanthinker.com/blog/2020/08/leftists_go_after_two_plus_two_equals_four.htm.

It's mind-blowing to study this stuff, but it only makes sense if you understand the motives. It makes sense when you look at the Political Identity Matrix:

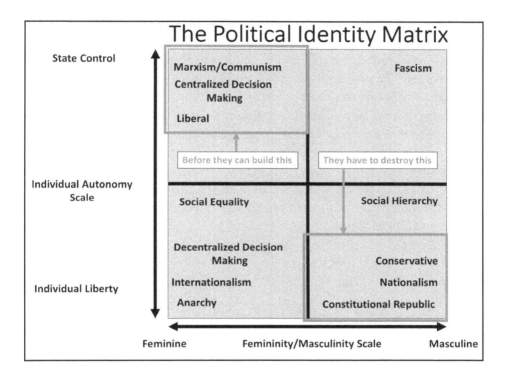

The "woke" religion of the left is designed to confuse, divide, and destroy but not to build anything. The war on truth is a key part of the strategy to confuse, divide, and destroy.

Today, you have to be more careful than ever to verify anything you hear from anyone. There are very practical consequences to living in a post-truth era. For example, do you want your doctor to prescribe you a lethal overdose because someone involved in the process was not taught to do the math correctly? Lies have consequences, and they can still be believed by a majority. In a post-truth era, you must be careful to verify sources and information that you may have safely accepted at face value in the past.

Limited Value of Debate

Attempting to debate someone committed to building the New World Order usually goes like this: decent people engage with indecent people in a decent manner, expecting to be treated decently in return and become very frustrated. Let's look at why.

Some debate strategies are highly effective but unethical. "Ad hominem" is a Latin word that means "against the man." An ad hominem argument is often preceded by a couple of other debate strategies—the lie and the label. If you attempt to debate in order to support a biblical position, be prepared to be subjected to any number of lies used to put one of the favorite labels on you—misogynist, homophobe, feminist hater, etc. They will try to quickly put you in the "label jail" we described earlier. Then your opponent will attempt to disqualify you from ever being correct about any belief or statement you hold that is contrary to theirs.

Love is often more powerful than debate in changing the way someone thinks. Debate can be a big timewaster because the truth stands alone, but the number of lies is theoretically infinite.

> In his book *Rules for Radicals*, Saul Alinsky, the original radical community organizer and societal change agent, says you should never have a rational discussion with your opponent. Doing so would humanize him, and your goal is to demonize him. With this tactic, he states that you can incur your opponent's wrath, causing him to respond angrily, and in many cases, irrationally, which then provides an opportunity to use that irrational response against him.[65]

---

[65] Ben Carson, "CARSON: Outgrowing Alinsky-style name-calling." October 2, 2013, https://www.washingtontimes.com/news/2013/oct/2/carson-outgrowing-alinsky-style-name-calling/.

Here are a few other things to keep in mind about dealing with leftists (actually upper left in the Political Identity Matrix):

1) To them, the end always justifies the means.
2) Their endgame is usually secret.
3) They have no moral boundaries.
4) Hypocrisy is a virtue to them since, to them, it is just a tool used to accomplish their goals.
5) In their words, "The issue is never about the issue. The issue is always about the revolution."

Most of these people are not interested in a fair debate anyway. Their endgame is censoring all sources of biblical truth.

Value Your National Identity

As more and more people have outsourced their consciences to the MSM (mainstream media), the MSM has been able to accomplish a psychological operation of turning "nationalism" into a dirty word. It's like convincing someone to hate their own house in the middle of a storm. Since I have shown you that the endgame of Satan is a totalitarian "New World Order," it should make more sense to you why nations, especially relatively decentralized western nations, are an obstacle to the goal of building a New World Order. I am a White male who was born in the United States. But if I moved to Kenya, I would immediately become a Kenyan nationalist, at least to the degree that the government supports individual human rights.

The other trend that is occurring in lockstep with the demonization of the concept of nationalism is the trend of trying to build "safe spaces" and completely separate nations inside the United States (as advocated by some of the "identity" religions). Of course, they don't think they can make it work without "reparations." All these trends are variations on the Hegelian "divide and conquer" strategy.

It doesn't take too much analysis to see how delusional and suicidal these trends are. The chart below shows some metrics of national strength broken down by nation:

	Population	GDP	Debt per capita (in $)	Masculinity Index	Incarceration Rate
	(higher is stronger)	(higher is stronger)	(lower is stronger)	(higher is stronger)	(lower is stronger)
China	1,433,783,686	13,608,152	1,326	66	120
India	1,366,417,754	2,726,323	383	56	34
United States	329,064,917	20,494,100	62,000	62	655
Indonesia	270,625,568	1,042,173	1,300	46	99
Pakistan	216,565,318	312,570	525	50	38
Brazil	211,049,527	1,868,626	3,200	49	348
Nigeria	200,963,599	397,270	60	46	36
Bangladesh	163,046,161	274,025	160	-	52
Russia	145,872,256	1,657,554	3,700	-	363
Mexico	127,575,529	1,223,809	3,300	69	163

Table 28. Strength metrics of most powerful nations.

In past decades, the United States has clearly been the strongest nation in the world. However, from an overall military and economic strength standpoint, things have radically changed. China has over four times the population of the United States, with far lower debt and a far lower incarceration rate. India has a population that rivals China, and the economic metrics are steadily trending higher. If China were to conquer or merge with India, it would take an alliance of the next twenty-one nations to equal the combined population of China and India. Fantasy theologies (such as the Black Hebrew Israelites and Hebrew Nation Building) that passive-aggressively harm the western nations they live in might as well be supported by the KGB or Chinese intelligence. Groups like Antifa and subsidized college campuses that try to create "safe spaces" seem to have the delusional and feminized idea that if foreign soldiers march in, all they have to do is shout, "We are on your side!" be "nice," and every-thing will be fine. The bottom line is whatever nation you choose to live in, you should patriotically support it and actively work to make it a better nation. Anything else is not only suicidal but is tacitly helping Satan, and those working for him, to build the New World Order.

Pray for Our Nation

We have been at a point for some time where we desperately need to apply II Chronicles 7:14.

> And My people who are called by my name humble themselves and pray and seek my face and turn from their wicked ways, then I will hear from heaven, will forgive their sin and will heal their land.

As we discussed earlier, we are called to proclaim the truth, but debating your enemies is of limited value. That may be because we often try to respond to the demonic with logic. We all should pray for our enemies instead of heading to an internet platform to debate them.

If you are a man, do what you can to organize groups of men to pray together for families, churches, and our nation. If you are a woman, do what you can to do the same thing with groups of women. There is something powerful about praying in a group.

> For where two or three have gathered together in My name, I am there in their midst. (Matthew 18:20)

Hold the Line

You now know that your enemies are trying to get you trapped in a Hegelian compromise loop, where they continue to attack while hoping that you continue to be "nice" and compromise. There is only one way to counter that attack—never give an inch.

Defend the lines of sex/gender, family definition, nation, Christian/non-Christian, etc. Don't be surprised if a "woke mob" tries to cancel you for saying something as innocuous as "I support traditional marriage."

Do not participate in interfaith dialogue. Remember, they only want the outcome of a debate or discussion to change you, not them.

Use the Identity Matrices to Analyze Objectives and Motives

People will often use innocent-sounding words and actions that appear harmless but are, in fact, weaponized. You can use both the Personal and Political Identity Matrices to help you determine the real objectives and motives of the latest tweet or political statement. Evaluate what direction on the Personal Identity Matrix and the Political Identity Matrix people are trying to move you. This will help you more quickly identify a wolf in sheep's clothing.

Another advantage of using the Political Identity Matrix is that instead of trying to unravel complicated conspiracies to figure out a person's true motives, you can use the matrix to evaluate the overall vector of their actions.

Advocate Decentralization

The Swiss psychologist Carl G. Jung stated, "The larger the organizations, the more inevitable are their immorality and blind stupidity."

Any centralized organization tends to funnel money and resources upward to the highest levels of leadership. Then there is a temptation for those leaders to fight for those resources and use them for personal gain. It is hypocritical for Marxists to talk about wanting to help oppressed people groups while advocating centralized government, which tends to be inherently oppressive. We recently saw one of the leaders of BLM, who admits to being a trained Marxist, have to step down after using BLM money to buy at least one mansion. Some of the last churches in the United States that have the courage to operate according to the Bible are independent. Once high levels in a centralized denomination are corrupted, it usually trickles down and corrupts the local churches. The chart below shows some important entities and institutions and shows both their centralized form and the decentralized form of their structure.

	Centralized	Decentralized
Population	City	Towns, Farms
Church	Denomination	Independent
Healthcare	Socialized Medicine	Cash Payment
Money	Electronic Chip (Beast)	Silver, Gold
Banking	Central Bank	Local Bank
Government	Global Marxism/Fascism	National Republic
Police	National Police	Local Police
Education	Public Education	Homeschooling
Utilities	On-grid	Off-grid
Transportation	Train	Car
Information	Electronic	Books
Social	Online	In-person
Communication	Cellphone	In-person
Entertainment	Television	Books, DVD's
Food	Supermarkets	Gardening, Farming, Hunting

Table 29 Centralized versus decentralized institutions

An example of decentralizing authority occurred in the first book of the Bible.

It came about the next day that Moses sat to judge the people, and the people stood about Moses from the morning until the evening. Now when Moses's father-in-law saw all that he was doing for the people, he said, "What is this thing that you are doing for the people? Why do you alone sit as judge and all the people stand about you from morning until evening?" Moses said to his father-in-law, "Because the people come to me to inquire of God. When they have a dispute, it comes to me, and I judge between a man and his neighbor and make known the statutes of God and His laws." Moses's father-in-law said to him, "The thing that you are doing is not good. You will surely wear out, both yourself and these people who are with you, for the task is too heavy for you; you cannot do it alone. Now listen to me: I will give you counsel, and God be with you. You be the people's representative before God, and you bring the disputes to God, then teach them the statutes and the laws, and make known to them the way in which they are to walk and the work they are to do. Furthermore, you shall select out of all the people able men who fear God, men of truth, those who hate dishonest gain; and you shall place these over them as leaders of thousands, of hundreds, of fifties and of tens. Let them judge the people at all times; and let it be that every major dispute they will bring to you, but every minor dispute they themselves will judge. So it will be easier for you, and they will bear the burden with you. If you do this thing and God so commands you, then you will be able to endure, and all these people also will go to their place in peace." So Moses listened to his father-in-law and did all that he had said. Moses chose able men out of all Israel and made them heads over the people, leaders of thousands, of hundreds, of fifties and of tens. They judged the people at all times; the difficult dispute they would bring to Moses, but every minor dispute they themselves would judge. Then Moses bade his father-in-law farewell, and he went his way into his own land. (Genesis 18:13–27)

The institution that is in the most need of decentralization is the church. You need to really think and pray about whether you should belong to a large denomination or a megachurch. They are simply too susceptible to being corrupted at the top, then the corruption trickles down. The other issue is that the "too big to fail" mindset creeps in so that the leadership will compromise on almost anything to try to please everybody and maintain unity.

One of the dangers of centralization in business is the monopoly. Monopolies ultimately harm consumers. They always do, at least from a value standpoint. Facebook, Google, Amazon, Twitter, and other platforms have an inordinate influence on what people think, say, do, and buy. Do your best to support your local small business and get off of social networking.

CHAPTER 14

Points to Remember

I want to reiterate a few things for emphasis:

1) The Bible uses the term "born again" to refer to salvation. This is one of many examples in the Bible of your "spiritual identity" being far more important than your "physical identity." This is your primary identity.

2) God designed men and women differently. God also mandated different roles for men and women. This is your secondary identity.

3) The theory of evolution is now treated as a law in our public school system. No debate with a creationist is allowed. One of the foundational tenets of the theory of evolution is survival of the fittest. All equality and equity efforts fly in the face of the survival of the fittest.

4) If you want to destroy something, feminize it first.

5) Cowardice will buy you time, but it will not buy you victory.

6) A lot of people are trying to do good things to save our culture, but the missing force multiplier is that we are not developing masculine Christian men.

The recent bashing of "Christian Nationalism," "White Christian Nationalism," etc., shows that the enemy understands the importance of marginalizing Christians in order to build the evil end goal of a global totalitarian state.

Support These Organizations

We are blessed to still have some courageous para-church organizations that are standing up to the satanic forces that are trying to deceive and destroy. Here is a list of some that, as of today, are worthy of support:

- Trail Life
- Family Research Council / frc.org
- Artofmanliness.com
- Ironmanoutdoors.org
- Inhisimage.org
- thechristianworldview.org
- Itsgoodtobeaman.org
- Afa.net

You Are under Surveillance

Oppressive governments use surveillance as a tool of oppression. Surveillance is used to detect and eliminate all opposition to the oppressor. In general, the higher the level of surveillance, the higher the level of tyranny. The based-on-a-true-story movie *Snowden* does a good job of revealing the level of surveillance we are all living under. The "real-life" reason Edward Snowden had to seek asylum in Russia was his discovery and revelation of the fact that the surveillance tools of CIA, FBI, and NSA are being used far more often to spy on US citizens than on foreign threats.

Cell phones, license plates, facial recognition identification cameras, Google, Facebook, credit card activity, and even the RFID chip in the key fob in your pocket or purse can be used to track your every move. Surveillance is a dangerous tool for oppression. You need to take measures to limit your vulnerability to surveillance in order to limit your potential to be oppressed.

Most Americans seem to understand that they are under surveillance, and nobody thinks it is a good thing. Yet every day, millions of United States citizens voluntarily hand over personal information about themselves on Facebook, Twitter, Instagram, etc. It is a testament to how social media has been engineered to be addictive, and the addiction is real. I highly recommend you unplug from these surveillance platforms. However, if you do decide to stay on, the less you post, the better. The other factor to keep in mind is that these platforms push narratives they want to promote and censor everything they are against. That means that you and your children are not just checking in on their friends, but you are all plugging into a sophisticated propaganda machine. If your children are on social media, there is a good chance that they are being told messages that contradict what you are trying to teach them.

In his book *Technocracy: The Hard Road to World Order*, Patrick M. Wood recommends some ways you can change to some safer platforms for your communication:

	Not Safe	Safer
E-mail	Gmail	ProtonMail.com
	Outlook	StartMail.com
		HushMail.com
Text Messaging and Phone Calls	Messages	Signal.org
	iMessage	
	WeChat	
Browsers	Chrome	Opera.com
	Edge	Brave.com
		EpicBrowser.com
Search Engines	Google	DuckDuckGo.com
	Bing	StartPage.com

Table 30. Platform options to avoid surveillance.

Final Thought

I discovered through my research in writing this book that the presence of masculine Christian men and feminine Christian women are the antidotes to many of the ills in our society. I challenge you to take what you have learned in this book to transform yourself, your family, your church, and your culture. If you properly identify with Christ, you will understand, like the disciples in the book of Acts, *that your message is more important than you are.*

BIBLIOGRAPHY

"7 Startling Facts: An Up Close Look at Church Attendance in America." *Outreach Magazine*. May 4, 2018. https://churchleaders.com/pastors/pastor-articles/139575-7-startling-facts-an-up-close-look-at-church-attendance-in-america.html.

Angelucci, Marc. "Men's Rights Issues." https://ncfm.org/know-the-issues/mens-rights-issues/.

"A Southern Baptist Seminary Professor Promotes Liberation Theology?" 2018. https://enemieswithinthechurch.com/2019/08/09/a-southern-baptist-seminary-professor-promotes-liberation-theology/.

"Autism Statistics and Facts." https://www.autismspeaks.org/autism-statistics-asd.

Bedford, Christopher. "'Blessings of Liberty:' How 'the Equality Act' Viciously Attacks Christians, Freedom, Society, Sex, and You." February 25, 2021. https://thefederalist.com/2021/02/25/blessings-of-liberty-how-the-equality-act-viciously-attacks-christians-freedom-society-sex-and-you/.

"BOMBSHELL: 'Justice Democrats' Founder is the Organizer of Evangelical Social Justice Movement." July 29, 2019. https://pulpitandpen.org/2019/07/29/bombshell-justice-democrats-founder-is-the-organizer-of-evangelical-social-justice-movement/.

Bosker, Bianca. "Why Witchcraft Is on the Rise." March 2020 issue. https://www.theatlantic.com/magazine/archive/2020/03/witchcraft-juliet-diaz/605518/.

Bratcher, Dennis. "Ba'al Worship in the Old Testament." May 20, 2016. http://www.crivoice.org/baal.html.

Brown, Michael. "HGTV and 'Throuple:' Mindlessly Careening Our Way Down the Slippery Slope." February 18, 2020. https://www.christianpost.com/voices/hgtv-and-throuple-mindlessly-careening-our-way-down-the-slippery-slope.html.

Carson, Ben. "CARSON: Outgrowing Alinsky-style Name-calling." October 2, 2013. https://www.washingtontimes.com/news/2013/oct/2/carson-outgrowing-alinsky-style-name-calling/.

Couronne, Ivan. "Patriot Act's Unintended Consequences in Post-9/11 World." January 12, 2015. https://news.yahoo.com/patriot-acts-unintended-consequences-post-9-11-world-203913740.html.

DeMar, Gary. *Ruler of the Nations*. Fort Worth, Texas: Dominion Press, 1987.

Dennison, Jim. "The Equality Act: What Christians Need to Know." February 26, 2021. https://www.denisonforum.org/resources/the-equality-act-what-christians-need-to-know/.

Dindyal, S. "The Sperm Count Has Been Decreasing Steadily for Many Years in Western Industrialized Countries: Is There an Endocrine Basis for This Decrease?" The Internet Journal of Urology, 2003.

"DISGUSTING: Black Lives Matter Mob Harasses and Attacks Church Members in Troy, New York." July 6, 2020. https://therightscoop.com/disgusting-black-lives-matter-mob-harasses-and-attacks-church-members-in-troy-new-york/.

Duffy, Evita. "White Supremacist Who Organized Charlottesville Race Riots Endorses Joe Biden." August 24, 2020. https://thefederalist.com/2020/08/24/white-supremacist-who-organized-charlottesville-race-riots-endorses-joe-biden/.

Emmons, Libby. "VILE: How to Be an Anti-racist Author Tweets Super Racist Smear of Amy Coney-Barrett." September 26, 2020. https://thepostmillennial.com/vile-how-to-be-an-anti-racist-author-tweets-super-racist-smear-of-amy-coney-barrett.

Erickson, Erick, and Bill Blankschaen. *You Will be Made to Care*. Washington, DC: Regnery Publishing, 2016.

Federal Bureau of Prisons. May 22, 2021. https://www.bop.gov/about/statistics/statistics_inmate_gender.jsp.

"Four Important Things to Know about the Black Hebrew Israelites." https://pulpitandpen.org/2019/12/13/four-important-things-to-know-about-the-black-hebrew-isr.

Garris, Zachary M. *Masculine Christianity*. Ann Arbor, Michigan: Zion Press, 2020.

Hahn, Jason Duaine. "Aaron Rodgers Opens Up about Religion to Danica Patrick: 'I Don't Know How You Can Believe in a God.'" Last modified January 22, 2020. https://people.com/sports/aaron-rodgers-opens-up-about-religion-to-danica-patrick-i-dont-know-how-you-can-believe-in-a-god/.

Hall, J. D. "Tim Keller Is a Marxist: A Response to Carl Trueman." October 9, 2018. https://pulpitandpen.org/2018/10/09/tim-keller-is-a-marxist-a-response-to-carl-trueman/.

Hendershot, Anne. "A Disturbing Guide to the Devilish Karl Marx." catholicworldreport.com, August 17, 2020.

Howse, Brannon S. *Marxianity*. Collierville, Tennessee: Worldview Weekend Press, 2018.

Howse, Brannon. "The Marxianity of Tim Keller and His Gospel Coalition." January 16, 2019. https://www.worldviewweekend.com/news/article/marxianity-tim-keller-his-gospel-coalition.

Howe, Neil. "You're Not the Man Your Father Was." October 2, 2017. https://www.forbes.com/sites/neilhowe/2017/10/02/youre-not-the-man-your-father-was/?sh=1afab9bf8b7f.

https://www.merriam-webster.com/.

https://www.patheos.com/blogs/geneveith/2018/12/destruction-of-the-boy-scouts/.

Inglis-Arkell, Esther. "The Frozen Calm of Normalcy Bias." May 2, 2013. https://io9.gizmodo.com/the-frozen-calm-of-normalcy-bias-486764924.

"Inside Largest US Gang: Rules, Lingo, Secrets." May 19, 2017. https://www.wyff4.com/article/inside-largest-us-gang-rules-lingo-secrets/9873763.

WILLIAM WELLINGTON

Jay, Anthony, PhD. "Estrogeneration: How Estrogenics Are Making You Fat, Sick, and Infertile." Tallahassee, Florida.

Jaye, Cassie. *The Red Pill*. DVD, directed by Cassie Jaye, Nena Jaye, Anna Laclergue, New York: ProSiebenSat.1 Media2016.

Kengor, Paul. "The Left's War on Boy Scouts Has Raged for 100 Years." June 1, 2018. https://www.westernjournal.com/the-lefts-war-on-the-boy-scouts-has-raged-for-100-years/.

Kim, Anthony B., and Julia Howe. "Why Democratic Socialists Can't Legitimately Claim Sweden or Denmark as Success Stories." August 10, 2018, eBook, Heritage Foundation.

Kimball, Linda. "Hegel's Dialectic: Erasing Christianity through the Psycho-Political 'Consensus Process.'" March 15, 2010. http://www.renewamerica.com/columns/kimball/100315.

"List of Countries Ranked by Ethnic Diversity Level." https://en.wikipedia.org/wiki/List_of_countries_ranked_by_ethnic_and_cultural_diversity_level.

Loudon, Trevor. "Marxist Critical Race Theory Infiltrates Churches, the Culture." August 8, 2019. https://www.theepochtimes.com/marxist-critical-race-theory-infiltrates-churches-the-culture_2983991.html.

Luther, Daisy. "Communists starving people." In *Prepper's Pantry*. New York, New York: Racehorse Publishing, 2019.

"Marxism, Postmodernism, and Critical Race Theory." June 18, 2020. https://gentlereformation.com/2020/06/18/marxism-postmodernism-and-critical-race-theory/.

Merkle, Rebekah. *Eve in Exile and the Restoration of Femininity*. Moscow, Idaho: Canonpress, 2016.

Miller, Eric C. "The Radical Rise of Liberation Theology: An Interview with Lilian Calles Barger." September 25, 2018. https://religionandpolitics.org/2018/09/25/the-radical-rise-of-liberation-theology-an-interview-with-lilian-calles-barger/.

Munro, Neil. "WSJ: Elites Enthusiasm for Transgenderism Endangers Gay, Lesbian Youth." February 15, 2020. https://www.breitbart.com/politics/2020/02/15/wsj-elites-enthusiasm-for-transgenderism-endangers-gay-lesbian-youth/.

New American Standard Bible (all Bible quotes).

"Normalcy Bias." https://en.wikipedia.org/wiki/Normalcy_bias.

Orwell, George. *Nineteen Eighty-Four*. Berkley, New York, New York: Harcourt Brace and Company, 1949.

Perkins, Tony. "Equality Act Assails Religious Freedom." April 1, 2021. https://www.frc.org/get.cfm?i=PV21D04

Pickle, Rober. "Sharia and Talmudic Law Not Compatible with Christianity." August 9, 2016. https://noahidenews.com/2016/08/09/sharia-and-talmudic-law-not-compatible-with-christianity/.

Podles, Leon. *The Church Impotent: The Feminization of Christianity*. Spence Publishing Company, Dallas, Texas, 75202, 1999.

Polk, Jennifer. "The Diminishing Dad," June 15, 2019, https://amgreatness.com/2019/06/15/the-diminishing-dad/.

Quaglia, Sofia. "Women Are Invoking the Witch to Find Their Power in a Patriarchal Society." October 31, 2019. https://qz.com/1739043/the-resurgence-of-the-witch-as-a-symbol-of-feminist-empowerment/.

"Rebecca McLaughlin: Gospelizing Idolatry at TGC Part II." 2018. https://enemieswithinthechurch.com/2019/05/07/mclaughlin-2/.

Roach, David. February 14, 2018. https://www.brnow.org/news/LGBTQ-hiring-policy-highlights-CBF-factions/.

Rufo, Christopher. "Critical Race Theory: What It Is and How to Fight It." March 2021. https://imprimis.hillsdale.edu/critical-race-theory-fight/.

Sandlin, P. Andrew. "Cultural Marxism, Simply Explained." April 23, 2018. https://docsandlin.com/2018/04/23/cultural-marxism-simply-explained/.

Sawyer, Wendy, and Peter Wagner. "Mass Incarceration: The Whole Pie 2020." Last modified March 24, 2020, https://www.prison-policy.org/reports/pie2019.html.

Segars, Catherine. December 11, 2020. https://www.crosswalk.com/faith/women/is-it-possible-to-be-a-christian-and-a-modern-feminist.html.

Smith, John C. P. "Does God Have a Gender?" June 3, 2020. https://answersingenesis.org/who-is-god/does-god-have-gender/.

Stanton, Glenn T. *Loving My (LGBTQ) Neighbor*. Moody Publishers, 2014, Chicago, Illinois.

"The Black Hebrew Israelite Cult, Exposed!" https://descendant-sofnoahh.wordpress.com/2015/04/26/the-black-hebrew-israelite-cult-exposed/.

"The Black Supremacist Democrats of 'Black Twitter' Should Discuss 2-Parent Homes." March 11, 2021. https://lovebreedsaccount-ability.com/2021/03/11/the-black-supremacist-democrats-of-black-twitter-should-discuss-2-parent-homes/.

"The Deep State Takedown of the Boy Scouts of America." February 19, 2018. https://www.scottlively.net/2020/02/19/the-deep-state-takedown-of-the-boy-scouts-of-america/.

"The Worship of Semiramis." https://aletheia.consultronix.com/7.html.

Tillison, Tom. "BLM Protesters Who Stormed NY Church Services Were Led by City Employee with Violent Criminal Past, Reports Say." July 7, 2020. https://www.bizpacreview.com/2020/07/07/blm-protesters-who-stormed-ny-church-services-were-led-by-city-employee-with-violent-criminal-past-943863/.

Tomassi, Rollo. *The Rational Male*: *Religion*. Counterflow Media, Reno, Nevada, 2020.

Vander Laan, Ray. "The Fertility Cults of Canaan." https://www.thattheworldmayknow.com/fertility-cults-of-canaan.

Vesper, H. W., Wang, Y., Vidal, M., Botelho, J. C., and S. P. Caudill. "Serum Total Testosterone Concentrations in the US Household Population from the NHANES 2011–2012 Study Population." Clin Chem 61, 2015, 1495–1504

"WATCH: BLM Activists Attack a Black Family as They Attempt to Enter Church in NY." July 2020. https://en-volve.com/2020/07/06/watch-blm-activists-attack-a-black-family-as-they-attempt-to-enter-church-in-nyc/.

"WATCH: BLM Activists Attack a Black Family as They Attempt to Enter Church in NYC." July 2020. https://en-volve.

com/2020/07/06/watch-blm-activists-attack-a-black-family-as-they-attempt-to-enter-church-in-nyc/.

"What Is the Fraud Triangle?" Corporate Finance Institute. https://corporatefinanceinstitute.com/resources/knowledge/accounting/fraud-triangle/.

Williams, Walter. "The Demonizing of White Men." dailysignal.com, 1/30/2019.

Wood, Patrick M. *Technocracy: The Hard Road to World Order*. Mesa, Arizona: Coherent Publishing, 2018.

Wurmbrand, Richard. *Marx and Satan*. Westchester, Illinois: Crossway Books.

ABOUT THE AUTHOR

William Wellington is the pen name of a Christian grandfather who deeply cares about the world we are leaving to our children and grandchildren. He has degrees in engineering and business and has worked for several major corporations in a variety of roles.

CPSIA information can be obtained
at www.ICGtesting.com
Printed in the USA
JSHW022100150323
39008JS00001B/41